ALSO BY DONALD KATZ

Just Do It: The Nike Spirit in the Corporate World

The Big Store: Inside the Crisis and Revolution at Sears

*Home Fires: An Intimate Portrait of One Middle-Class Family
in Postwar America*

The King of the Ferret Leggers and Other True Stories

The Valley of the Fallen

and Other Places

DONALD KATZ

THE VALLEY OF THE FALLEN AND OTHER PLACES

NEW YORK

AtRandom.com Books and colophon are registered trademarks of Random House, Inc.

Library of Congress Cataloging-in-Publication Data

Katz, Donald R.
The valley of the fallen and other places / Donald Katz.
p.   cm.
ISBN 0-8129-9182-6 (tbp. : alk. paper)
I. Title.

PN4874.K35 A25 2001b
814'.6—dc21   2001035548

Website address: www.atrandom.com

Printed in the United States of America on acid-free paper

2 4 6 8 9 7 5 3

First Edition

TO MY MOTHER,

WITH LOVE

Contents

Introduction

It is entirely possible that I could have spent the 20-year expanse from which these stories are drawn working as a lawyer or a teacher, but thanks to the cooperation of Francisco Franco, I was lucky enough to become a wandering writer of nonfiction prose. I wrote the first article in this volume in 1975, when I was 23 years old. At the time I was a graduate student who loved Faulkner novels. I was living in England and studying European politics and economics. I wrote a two-page letter to the editors of *Rolling Stone* magazine offering my literary services, though I had no previously published writing to show for myself. In the letter I posited that a good story might be spun from local observation of the last days of the aging Spanish dictator, particularly if the story could be told from the viewpoint of the colorful Basque nationalists I had encountered during a month living near the French-Spanish border. The Basques I knew were associated with the ETA underground movement, and they all hated Franco and his regime with a religious passion. Their perceptions were so much at odds with standardized journalistic accounts of contemporary Spain that I wondered if something interesting—or more dramatic, or more accurate or even more truthful—could be wrought from trying to present a different perspective on Spain at the edge of an era.

Within weeks after I sent the letter, Franco entered a hospital in Madrid, where he was expected to die any day. I got a telegram from *Rolling Stone*: "Go to Spain. Write 5,000 words. We will pay $1,500 and pay reasonable expenses."

The Spanish dictator's many weeks of dying during that autumn of 1975 brought about something of a reunion for dozens of European-based foreign correspondents who were nearing the end of their long careers. Many of them had come together with regularity for much of the post–World War II era to cover the passing of midcentury leaders and other matters of state. In bars, in wire-service offices, and at innumerable press conferences in and around Madrid, several of these reporters showed me what reporters did. They taught me how to obtain press credentials, where to find out about official events, and where to stand in a crowd. But I was consistently struck by the incongruous juxtaposition of the reporters' rich late-night storytelling—they were so knowing and had seen so much of the world and could spin such riveting tales—and the heavily circumscribed news copy they would churn out each day in deference to the rules of their profession.

I began to travel back and forth between the Basque region and the premourning formalities back in Madrid, and so commenced a process of straddling the world of underground resistance and entrenched policy elites that would mark the early years of my journalistic career. The underground/elites dichotomy was underscored when, a few weeks after "Dispatch from the Valley of the Fallen" was published in *Rolling Stone,* I got a phone call from a man who identified himself as Martin Peretz, a Harvard professor who had just purchased the storied journal *The New Republic*. Peretz asked me to be a London-based contributor to his magazine. The next day I went to the office of the director of the London School of Economics and told her I was leaving her Ph.D. program because I'd found a job.

Many of the stories in this collection—like many of the eleven stories about people published a few months ago in my collection *The King of the Ferret Leggers and Other True Stories*—convey the ambivalence about the interplay of good storytelling and solid reportage that had first emerged in Spain. The challenge of nonfiction, I thought, was to find real situations possessed of underlying psychological, moral, historical, and dramatic components compelling enough to inform a novel or short story. I was certainly not the only young writer of that time who turned to feature writing with an awareness of the distance between the fiction of Bellow, Roth, Mailer, Styron, and other writers and the "just the facts" prose in contemporary newspapers. Many emerging writers of the moment, and even more readers, also harbored a general mistrust of straight-ahead journalism, because, during the Vietnam War and the American civil rights movement, apparently authoritative reporting had too often been untrue.

I began to career from country to country during the early years of my career, as middle-class terrorism and Third World wars of liberation dominated the news, and I came to believe that good nonfiction stories could only be "true" if they included what Henry James once described as the key element of the novel, "direct impressions of life." I would seek out people who were set within, or against, their places and times. How did it feel to pick up a gun and enter the swirl of history? What was it that pushed certain individuals to the decision that there was indeed something worth dying for? When I was on the scene amid the carnage of the Ethiopian Red Terror, running with the pre–Red Brigade gangs in Italy, or reconsidering police killings of civilians in Houston, editors would allow me to watch and wait until circumstances delivered up a guide, a character who could walk both writer and reader through elements of the story. The theme of "people and place" also encompassed an anthropological fascination with obsessive pastimes that had emerged from the history of various regions. In that vein, this volume includes a look at the art of skating for miles along frozen canals in Holland and an examination of the practice in the American South of catching gigantic catfish by plunging one's hands down the powerful prehistoric throats of the fish.

Part II of this book includes some stories drawn from my subsequent focus on the dramas encased within economic life. Around the time I wrote "The Boys in the Pits" for *Esquire,* which dealt with financial madness in Chicago in the early 1980s, I began a six-year project writing *The Big Store*, a business narrative set inside Sears, Roebuck and Co. Within the political storms of that racked Sears, I hunted for the same kinds of obsessions and strangeness that had marked some of the violent political scenes I'd studied early on.

The novelist Mary Gordon once stated that "nonfiction is true when it is beautiful." I'd like to think nonfiction can aspire to beauty and even a complexity of design when it is true. My basement is stuffed with dozens of cardboard boxes filled with tapes, notebooks, reams of clippings, and thousands of pages of typed transcripts, because the trick was finding something compelling that was also true. I never thought a piece was successful if it reflected only a truth like the ones found in photography or cinematography. The idea was to try to assemble stories possessed of the kind of refracted truth of people and place that is revealed in paintings. I hope the pieces in this collection at least convey that aspiration. And for all of the hard work involved, I assume the stories will also suggest how very lucky I was to have borne witness to these pieces of recent history—and lucky to have stumbled into such a great job.

PART I

OTHER PARTS

DISPATCH FROM
THE VALLEY OF THE FALLEN

A man's dying is more the survivors' affair than his own.
—THOMAS MANN

The macabre series of tubes, pumps, wires, and clamps connected to Francisco Franco miraculously pulsed and wheezed throughout much of the month of November. In taking so very long in dying, Generalissimo Francisco Franco y Bahamonde, the *Caudillo de España,* by the very grace of God was effectively unweaving a great deal of the heavy matting which had held Spanish society in a political stasis for some 40 years.

Franco had sought to construct a society blessed by an apolitical serenity. Spain was to be an outpost of hope in a ridiculous world that still believed politics to be a matter of popular concern. But one of the wiliest and most vicious Machiavellis ever to wield a scepter was finally dying, and neither his 32 doctors nor the grace of God was going to save him.

Only six floors above Franco, in the very same hospital, another man lay near death. Juan Alberto Sevilla, a 25-year-old engineering student at the University of Madrid, had somehow survived ten days of inhuman torture at the hands of Spanish police. Many of his bones were severely broken; his face had been completely disfigured by hundreds of cigarette burns; his kidneys had ceased to function properly from being so barbarously stomped; and there was doubt as to whether he would ever leave the dialysis machine. His tongue had been all but burned out of his mouth.

After he had been missing for some eight days, authorities contacted Sevilla's family and said that Juan had been taken ill and was being treated. Under the new antiterrorist laws in Spain, an individual may be detained for ten days without being charged. Sevilla was never charged.

"He had been arrested before," his brother said in the lobby of the hospital, "but only for an hour or two. He wrote some light political commentary in the university-sanctioned student newspaper. We couldn't even get him to the hospital until we came up with a 200,000-peseta [about $3,400] fine." The brother was smiling. It was a common smile among the young of Spain; combining an awareness of impossible absurdities and a painful resignation to the immutability of their existence. Juan Sevilla was dying of a bad case of political repression.

—

Going south out of Bordeaux, in southwestern France, one finds that the flat Bordelais vineyards soon yield to the soft protuberances of the Basque hills. The Pyrenees roll in the distance as you work your way down the Côte Basque: past Bayonne, through Biarritz, St. Jean de Luz, then Hendaye and eventually to the Spanish border. This is the border between information, memories, and active political thought on one side, and a veritable political vacuum on the other.

Hundreds of thousands of Spaniards have been forced to live in France over the last 40 years. They are refugees from the Spanish Civil War, political exiles of Franco's regime or economic victims of the pervasive poverty of Spain during the fifties. They live in Toulouse, in the Quartier St. Michel in Bordeaux, and dominate the population of Bayonne. Some of them have never given up their citizenship of the Republic of Spain. They have waited 40 years for a change in the system that forced them to leave their homes.

Then there are the Basques: even the failing godling in Madrid is believed to fear the power of their will to independence. People here think about Franco often. This was the best vantage point from which to watch Franco die.

The smoldering political passions which lie under the beautiful landscape of this area became apparent during the summer of 1974. It was then that Franco suffered an acute attack of phlebitis (known officially in Madrid as "the crisis"), almost died but didn't ("the miracle"). While his condition worsened the bars and cafés in these towns and villages submitted the largest orders for extra liquor that the region had ever seen. Now they had waited more than a year to have that party.

It's a strangely beautiful area. The broad beaches are marked by massive German blockhouses from World War II. The French government tried to blow them up after the war but the thickness of the walls made the cost of demolition outweigh the immediate desire to rid the area of the ugly shrines.

Jay Gould, the notorious 19th-century American magnate, used to live here. So did Juan Carlos, Spain's new king, until someone told him that it was politically unwise to vacation in the area.

The famous city of Biarritz is considered off-limits to political activists, although there was a killing in the main street several months ago. The European rich still come to Biarritz in the summer to gamble in the casino or hit floating golf balls into a lake. Latter-day Hemingways stalk the streets looking for Sonny's Bar. It was closed last year. Only the scratches on the walls remind you that Biarritz is right in the middle of the Basque country. They say, "Franco au Garrot, Franco Assassin."

The most apparent change in a city like Bayonne, three miles north of Biarritz, is in the quality of the fear. Revenge, violent revenge, has become a way of life for some of the exiles and for all of the Basques. Old friends will talk only if names are never used. Some won't talk at all.

At dinner in Bayonne, the Spanish radio station announced that Franco had survived another operation and was rallying. An old man closed his eyes.

It had been a hell of a life. He had been jailed for his union activities in 1934 when the nascent Spanish Republic reacted to activities from the left. Then he had fought for three years for that republic against Franco, "bad years." Then three more years fighting Hitler as a member of the French underground—then ten months in Buchenwald. After that, he worked 30 years as a second-class citizen of a country he had never considered his own.

"You know that I only cried once," he said. "That was after I got the news about Potsdam. All that time I truly believed that the Allies would liberate Spain and empty the jails as they'd emptied the camps, but they didn't."

The conversation moved back to Franco: a few Franco jokes ensued. All Spaniards tell Franco jokes. None of them are funny. It's the iconoclasm of it all; like Pope jokes or dead baby jokes.

Someone noted that a doctor had said that Franco was dying a painful death, a bad death.

"Suffer!"

It was the daughter speaking. With an almost supplicant gaze she repeated it, hissing, *"Souffrez, souffrez, souffrez!"*

———

In a little village outside Bayonne, a group of Spanish workers assembled for one of their regular meetings. There are many groups like this in France now. Some of them are active Spanish Communist party militants, others are simply trying to maintain the cultural and political ties which bring them hope. Their numbers have been greatly swelled by the latest wave of arrests in Spain and the attendant fears of the Spanish left.

The discussion ranged from the American imperialistic presence in Spain, in the form of military bases and capital investment, to the expectations of the group for a new Spain after Franco:

"Power in Spain must now come from the united workers," a man said. "There are certain things which must come immediately, such as total amnesty. Otherwise it's to the streets."

"Yes," a woman named Carolina was saying, "but no more killing."

"No *more* killing?"

As the dialectical verbiage became increasingly boring, some of the emotions and memories began to emerge. Sitting around a small kitchen table with this woman, and with these big men with gigantic forearms and soiled hands, I sensed the mood change. Then the stories came. Carolina continued:

"You have to understand that in every Spanish family there is a drama of misery and poverty, scars from the Civil War. I was seven. My father had been killed by Franco's troops; my mother was dying in jail. My other relatives had fought for Franco. I had to live in the street and my uncles and cousins would walk by while I starved. I was little and didn't understand. Franco's system won't die, it must be killed, but too many of us remember the hunger." She clasped her hands as if to snap herself out of a daydream.

"Franco is dying," a man said, "now Francoism must follow."

———

Even the children carry a vivid picture of the Spanish Civil War. Every Spanish family absorbed a loss. Everyone has had a relative in prison. The war lasted for two and a half years after the day that a young general named Franco launched an attack on the Spanish Republican government.

Seven hundred thousand people lost their lives in battle, another 50,000 died in air raids. Some 400,000 people went into exile. They say that Franco held 300,000 in prisons after the war; by 1942 two-thirds of them had been executed or had died in prison.

The Civil War was the world's first chance to see its new weapons in action. Hitler tested his Stuka dive bombers and incendiary bombs on cities like Guernica. Mussolini sent in his tanks and more than 75,000 men. The war ended in total defeat for the Republic. Despite their repeated requests for a negotiated peace with the nationalists, Franco crushed them in the final months. Three thousand Americans fought in that war.

—

In Guernica the emotions have long since transcended verbal expression. Franco's condition brought back the memories. Guernica had been the capital of the short-lived independent Basque Republic before the bombing and the war; it still suggests some unfinished business for the powerful movement for Basque nationalism.

The Basque country includes four provinces in Spain and three in France. There are just over two million Basques, the great majority of whom still live in Spain. The enigma of their origins has had anthropologists theorizing for years. Some even believe them to be the Lost Tribe of Israel. The Basque language bears no resemblance to any extant spoken language. They even have a separate blood type.

Their present quest for national autonomy is particularly intimidating for Spanish authorities because of a variety of endemic abilities and traditions. For one thing, they are historically fierce and efficient fighters. For another, there is an established tradition of border running through the Pyrenees. For years, the Basques ran huge smuggling organizations over a variety of frontiers. It is a matter of pride. The border, they believe, is a phenomenon wrought by the French and Spanish and should thus have little effect on the Basques' ability to cross it. A bartender friend named Felipe crossed the border every weekend to see his girlfriend. When I asked him if the fact that there was a price on his head scared him, he laughed. That was a year ago. The Spanish police eventually arrested his girlfriend. Felipe gave himself up.

The recent spate of police violence in the Basque country has caused many of the more conservative Basques to support ETA, a separatist, paramilitary grouping of young Basques. The group has gained both fame and numbers since an ETA bomb blew Spanish president Admiral Luis Carrero Blanco to bits in December 1973. The urban underground in Spain considers ETA a bit primitive but there is a tacit respect for their unmitigated gall.

"You want to know something about that Carrero Blanco bomb?" This was a high-ranking ETA operative. Official permission had been granted for an interview.

"The international press all thought that the Russians were supplying us with sophisticated electronic detonation systems. It was just some guy standing there with a switch."

Throughout the period of Franco's illness, ETA had been surprisingly inactive. Late in September two of their members had been executed with three others for terrorist activities in Spain. The execution had international repercussions. It is common knowledge in the Basque country, and this is corroborated by journalists, that the fingerprints found in the car of the alleged terrorists bore no relationship to those of the five dead men. But still ETA waited. A two-day general strike was called in certain Basque regions but there was none of the usual vengeance. There is a reason:

"They have our people. We have been specifically warned that prisoners will be butchered the day that Franco dies if we resume activity. We can't do that. Besides, there is some hope for an amnesty after Franco is gone. We can wait."

There is also the recent offensive by right-wing terrorists on the ETA operatives in France. The Guerrillas of Christ the King (GCR) are a group of well-armed and suspiciously well-informed men who have launched up to 30 bombing and shooting attacks so far. The man who was authorized to speak for ETA had his entire café blown into the street last summer. A good friend of his was injured, as were his children, after a bomb exploded in their car on the morning of our first interview.

"What about the fear?"

His young son hung joyfully on his neck. He said something in Basque and the boy left.

"Whenever I get scared I think about the importance of it all." He threw a photograph of a gentle-looking man on the table top. "My brother. He was never involved in politics. He ran a little bar in Bilbao, worked hard, loved his family. All the Basques knew him. Then I was sentenced to 100 years in prison. After I escaped through the mountains, the GCR walked into his bar and killed him. It was just to get at me. Now what do you want to know about fear?"

The ETA chieftains estimate that there are as many as 3,000 active members now. Some of them are much too hot to enter Spain while others can't even show their faces in Bayonne. They still believe that they can rally a million Spanish Basques if necessary.

Their arms come from all over the world and from all sides of the political spectrum. Pistols from Spain itself, some explosives from Ireland and the Middle East, submachine guns from Czechoslovakia. They even make weapons at home.

The Basques feel so cut off from mainstream opposition politics that the Spanish left only nominally considers them viable members of a cohesive opposition. "I am simply not Spanish," one man intoned. "A little democracy in Spain will open things up for us. We are united with a group like FRAP [the Maoist underground urban units in Barcelona and Valencia] only insofar as we all hate Franco and his system. But I am Basque."

The radio in the corner reports that Franco needs a third operation. The odds are 100 to 1 against success. There are smiles all around. "Maybe tomorrow we drink champagne."

———

Just across the border is Irun. It is separated from the French city of Hendaye by only a narrow canal. The Spanish border guards have developed an expertise in picking off swimmers headed for France. Hendaye is of symbolic importance to the Spaniards. It is here that Franco met Hitler in 1940. There is a famous photograph of the two of them smiling knowingly.

At the airport in Irun a woman with the Basque name of Miranchu talks of the passive grace with which Spaniards are accepting the Caudillo's illness:

"All is calm here. There is no opposition. In 1936 everyone was hungry. You must understand the Spanish mentality." She points across the canal. "There you have trouble, the French. The economy is good here. All is calm. You won't find your violence to write about."

The economy, in fact, isn't in good shape. Unemployment has become a big problem despite laws forbidding layoffs. Inflation hovers at around 20 percent. Wage settlements were up by about 25 percent last year while production fell by more than 9 percent.

On November 12, Francisco Franco was having trouble breathing. They inserted another tube and began blowing in air to keep his lungs working.

On the same day, five ETA members were arrested in Pamplona. Three of them were women. Most ETA people winced at this news. The torture of women in the northern jails is especially cruel. There is a theory that many of the SS elite found refuge in Spain after the war; thus there is widespread use of drugs, electrical shocks, burning, and general mutilation.

Certain of these specialists have gained fame in the underground. One, an interrogator for the *brigada social,* the political police, is known as Billy the Kid. He has blond hair and looks to be around 12. His specialty is applying cigarettes to nipples. Milder treatment includes head shaving and old-fashioned bull-whipping. In October a man and a woman were thrown to their deaths out of a police station window in Bilbao.

The police activity in Spain began to pick up by mid-November. Nearly 500 official arrests had been made. Twenty people were accused under the antiterrorist laws, which carry an automatic death sentence after a trial that includes no real defense arguments. Two priests were arrested for telling their parishioners that it wasn't necessary to pray for Franco. Seven people were arrested in San Sebastian for "improper respect for the military authorities" after they protested the beating of a young boy.

By November 18, doctors had lowered Franco's temperature to the hibernation level to stop his internal bleeding. There was talk of freezing him for a few months. Three generals volunteered their hearts if that would help.

The fact that what was left of Franco was legally still alive started bizarre guessing games in the hospital lobby ("See that nose, it's the Caudillo"). Franco had used up enough blood to sustain ten other men and the hospital was running out of his type. His 32 doctors sedulously continued to keep him going.

——

So it persisted: the frustration and the fear of an interminable wait. He was going to take the fun out of it. It was going to be the last thing he ever did, but those who hated him would have to live with the possibility of his recovery for more than five weeks, and the ones who loved him would squirm too. They all worried and wondered about their future. Franco was going to show them all how much he'd meant to them.

The death of Francisco Franco was going to be the first substantive historical event for some 25 million of Spain's 35 million people. Amazingly, nothing had happened between 1939 and 1975 that in any way had an immediate effect on the lives of the Spanish people.

The programmatic yearnings of the various opposition groups on the left are noble, yet almost childlike in their idealism. The socialists are prepared to give monarchy a chance, while the highly organized Communist party demands free political parties and elections within 12 to 18 months.

The groups are presently converging around two political poles: the Junta Democratica, which is dominated by Communists, and the Convergencia Democratica, which is a rather amorphous mixture of social democrats, Christian democrats, and socialists. There is said to be a large number of politicized labor groups—but no one can see them. The all too obvious question is whether parties which are organizing on an electoral line can ever hope to budge a political system which has been unencumbered by a single general election for 44 years.

—

At 4:40 A.M. on November 20, Franco was dead. The American Armed Forces radio network solemnly announced a program of martial music. The old ones walked the streets of Madrid with tears in their eyes.

A woman on the street told me that her father was dead. An American correspondent looked at his article and said that the story had been ready for five years. In a note from the Caudillo which was read to the country on television, Franco asked forgiveness.

The body lay in state all day Friday and Saturday. On Friday, the Spanish government television network reported that millions of Spaniards were waiting in the cold to say goodbye. There weren't anywhere near that number in line. On Saturday, there *were* millions of Spaniards waiting to see the body. They knew what it meant to be a bad Spaniard and it really wasn't too cold to be a good one.

Porfirio Esteban, an 88-year-old war veteran, waited 12 hours in the dampness to pay his respects. As he approached the coffin, he stopped, stared at that hoary and wizened little face, snapped a violent fascist salute, and dropped dead—right there amid the marble and the glory. They carried him out and the line continued. It was the closest that most of these mourners had ever gotten to Franco.

Then everyone told the old stories. About how he'd executed a man for dirtying his uniform; about how no one could speak in a ministerial meeting; about his obsession with Napoleon. He went to Mass every night and always stood by his family. A large percentage of his daughter's assets has, it is said, been moved to the Philippines—just in case.

Upon examining the record, you have to admit that he wasn't a fascist—not analytically anyway. He never had a book. Technically, he was a conservative-nationalist dictator. He was also an accomplished manipulator of human beings, a brilliant tactician, and a student of the failings of the human spirit.

History may well show that he bore a similar relationship to his people as de Gaulle did to his. De Gaulle loved France but hated the French; and when they asked him what France would do when he was gone, he said that they would simply have to find another de Gaulle.

———

Back in Bayonne they were drunk. Every one of them was as drunk as any of them had ever been. It was that pervasive, saturated kind of total drunkenness that comes from drinking all day. The drink is some green fissionable material called Izzara, a Basque drink. They weren't so much dancing in the streets as rolling along the walls of the narrow alleyways. The noise was deafening, bouncing off the walls and coming out of the windows. The parties and the drunken café scenes spilled together in an effluvium of joy.

An ETA contact rolled up and just smiled, tried to talk, and then rolled on. A man was singing a song about the death of Carrero Blanco at the top of his lungs. That song would have got him killed on the other side of the border. Red, white, and green Basque flags flew defiantly from the homes in Hendaye.

They ran out of liquor across the border in San Sebastian, but theirs was a quieter and more determined kind of drunkenness. The streets were lined with hundreds of gray-coated Guardia Civil police. It was quiet. It had to be.

———

The day before the funeral an interview was arranged with two active anarchists in Madrid. The bulk of the guerrillas had cleared out of Madrid the day Franco died. These two men were scared and it was contagious. They ran down a series of statements that reeked of memorization.

They did say that they were part of a working group of about 40 people. Thirty others were in prison. That group was divided into smaller sections for weapons procurement, international contacts, and propaganda distribution.

Theirs is a syncretic form of anarchism in the old tradition of European radicalism. It is a violent fanaticism which can only survive in the aura of hate and oppression that has always accompanied totalitarianism. There is no support of any identifiable plank. "The political mentality of Spain has been castrated," one man said. "You don't patch that up immediately with a new system; the institutions and the system must go."

They wouldn't outline which specific activities they had been involved in previously but did say that bombing and assassination were part of the show. The rather hackneyed phrase "There are no innocents" sounded like a real threat here.

"There is only a loose confederation on the extreme left," the anarchist said. "The Catalonian groups are more cohesive. There is a large anarcho-syndicalist element in the labor movement. The problem is the ones you can't pin down, the anarcho-hippies."

Then he whispered, "There is a meeting at the beginning of December. I can't tell you who will be there but there is a meeting and its purpose is to discuss coordinated action."

His eyes were darting from side to side.

"Would you bomb the funeral tomorrow?"

"The funeral?" He looked at me as if I were crazy.

"Well, it would run with your line."

"Man, do you know that *Rockefeller* will be there?"

—

The famous Plaza Mayor was deserted by one o'clock that night, save for three policemen kicking the shit out of a drunk. In every alley or doorway where there wasn't a policeman, couples, some of them older than teenagers, stood necking in the shadows—a symptom of this most repressive of social orders.

And everywhere, but everywhere, there were guns. The entire Guardia Civil, the 85,000-man army that can only jokingly be considered a police force, had been issued lightweight, snub-nosed submachine guns. They stood at every corner, behind doors and on rooftops. They looked nervous and, worst of all, they pointed the damn things at your belly, and sometimes they smiled.

The Spanish authorities can be the most officious in the world. Their bureaucracies beget bureaucracies until the system itself has turned in on people's ability to act. Madrid is a city which oozes with the accoutrements of stability. When you make a religion of order, then the ministry becomes a temple and the police the priests.

When Pope Paul VI called the execution of five terrorists "murderous repression," he was censored.

To be a journalist from another country in Madrid you need a signed statement from virtually everyone you have ever known to get the proper credentials.

The Spanish media treat the Spanish people like a group of children. A minister recently gave an impassioned speech calling for more sports and less "destructive" education. The newspapers are all sanctioned and censored by the National Movement, the only legal party (though the word "party" is proscribed in Spain). Their format is usually based on equal parts of high society news and advertisement—with four pages of real news in the center.

On the day of Franco's funeral, one large Madrid daily included its regular Sunday color supplement. It included gossip about the relative fervency of Loretta Young's Catholicism, pictures of John Wayne with the Russian cosmonauts, and a three-page article entitled "What I Think of Sports" by Gerald Ford.

—

In the Basque country they call him *Juan Carlitos el Corto*—Juan the Brief. No one can ever say that the freshly dead paladin never left Spain a living legacy. He made them a king. Juan Carlos' credentials include the fact that he was a member of the 1972 Olympic sailing team; he was "King for a Month" in August 1974; he cuts ribbons beautifully; and he happened to be the personal tutee of Generalissimo Franco.

The elections of 1931 which brought a Republican government to power in Spain also deposed the Bourbon family of which Juan Carlos is a member. He says that his present mandate comes from a highly questionable national referendum held in 1974. In fact, it comes from Franco.

Juan Carlos was made king of Spain before the Spanish Cortes (parliament) the day before the funeral. He has a number of hurdles to jump before he'll acquire any semblance of security. His amnesty proposal is just the kind of thing that will stir up subliminal Spanish passions. By releasing any prisoner he will enrage the far right; by releasing only a few, he will incite the left. He has already dealt with the replacement of the speaker of the Cortes, an old Falangist named Alejandro Rodriguez de Valcarel. But his prime minister, Carlos Arias Navarro, remains. Like de Valcarel, he is a relic of Franco's "bunker," the rightist establishment.

Whether the institutions such as the military or the church will help Juan Carlos remains to be seen. Too much is unknown even to try to envisage a scenario. All that is known at this point is that he certainly looks like a king.

—

While thousands of people still waited in the street to catch a glimpse of the corpse, the coffin was moved to the Plaza de Oriente for an early morning Mass. People wept and waved white handkerchiefs. The sermon was short and sweet. At the end, the loudspeaker announced that the authorities were sorry but there would be no sacrament due to the size of the crowd. There was a moaning sound that droned throughout the assemblage.

Then the procession started. The burial was to be 35 miles away at the famous Valley of the Fallen. First came the motorcycles, then hundreds of horsemen with colorful capes and tall lances, then a formation of ludicrous-looking minibuses with piles of gaudy flowers sticking out the windows. And finally, sitting starkly on the back of a big flatbed military truck, the polished wooden coffin. As the crowds along the road pushed to get a glimpse, they started to cheer and yell, "Franco, Franco, Franco." A sword and a scepter were balanced precariously on the coffin.

At the Valley it was different. The people who waited outside the crypt had been there for much of the night. The road from Madrid was closed. An estimated 70,000 people stood in the wind. Here was the Falange. They stood in formation with their blue uniforms, black ties, and bright red berets. In the front were the old Camisas Azules, tattered old men who all appeared to have seen a day when they were strong and hard. They had fought with the Nazis during the war at Franco's request. One man told me so, hardly able to contain his pride.

There were children too. The young Fuerza Nueva, fascist troops of boys in shorts and the same red berets. They had been called from the countryside to honor their fallen leader—or so it seemed.

Everyone waited for Franco to arrive. A formation of priests and altar boys moved to a prominent rock and looked at the road. The priest held a ten-foot jeweled cross. The bitter wind lifted their white vestments to reveal skinny ankles.

This valley means a lot to Spanish fascists like the members of the Falange. Their leader, José Antonio Primo de Rivera, is buried in this very crypt.

Franco played Pharaoh in building this monument and he was completing the role by being buried here. It was built by captured Civil War prisoners. Countless numbers of them died while trying to bore the basilica some 1,000 feet into the rock face and while trying to construct the obscene 495-foot-high cross.

An overpowering paradox exists in this valley: with the 495-foot phallus, the fascist guard at the tomb of one real fascist and one megalomaniac, a place built by slaves—it is Godforsaken.

The entourage appeared in the distance. As the coffin approached, the moaning and droning of the morning's Mass resumed, but it was louder, much louder. The wind was whistling by at a good clip and helicopters hovering overhead added to the undertone. The Falangists started cheering and crying and snapping fascist salutes. When they picked up the coffin a man screamed over a microphone:

"EL CAUDILLO DE ESPAÑA!"

"PRESENTE!"

They all were thundering in response. The voice urged them again. In the background was a hoarse and painful "FRANCO, FRANCO, FRANCO, FRANCO." They all kept saluting and screaming and crying, then they broke into "Face of the Sun," their anthem, as the arms kept snapping into the sky like so many knives.

Then they moved simultaneously into an "ARRIIIIIBA FRANCO! ARRIIIIIBA FRANCO!" It was utterly deafening, overpowering. Suddenly it was clear. They were turning this man's funeral into a political field day. This was a rally at Nuremberg. A band suddenly struck up a march, hopelessly out of tune. One man yelled to another, "Franco would have had them shot."

When the noise hit its peak, the frenzy and the twirling and the tears and the memories, it was a bad eschatological Franco joke: The Caudillo was going to stand up all dripping with embalming fluid. He was going to mount that cross with tubes in his orifices, spit out some foam rubber, and yell, *"Viva España!"*

The chill didn't leave for days.

For years Franco had only called on this type of show of force by the Falange when he was in trouble. After the executions they had staged a rally in the Plaza de Oriente to support the generalissimo. These men see themselves the victors of a civil war that has to be fought forever. They are present in the government in great force although their dominance was seriously impaired by a 1969 cabinet reshuffle.

The real threat to peaceful change in Spain may well come from the right. The lunatic groups to the right of the Falange are numerous and active:

Fuerza Nueva is the most prominent. Its leader, Blas Piñar, is a powerful demagogue. Piñar hates capitalists, Marxists, religious freedom, and, if it helps our international ego any, Americans.

The Guerrillas of Christ the King are extremely restless. There is great fear of their attacking prisons in order to get at incarcerated leftists. They know that a right-wing military takeover can only occur if they help create the violence.

There are a variety of groups to the right of that. The PENS, the Spanish National Socialist party, specializes in attacking bookstores, students, and Jews. Another group, the CLA, specializes in attacking art galleries in order to get at the work of a famous political exile, Pablo Picasso.

If you are a king who seeks a modicum of change and you know that the right wing includes the mainstay of the army, all of its veterans, the wife of the former Caudillo, a group of young fanatics (many of whom are policemen during the day), and an 85,000-man paramilitary police force, you may know that you have more than a "conservative element" on your hands.

—

Watch Spain. She's an orphan now, a jaundiced political anachronism afloat in a time warp. Lassitude and ebullition are squaring off and their jaws are squeaking like the Tin Man's.

A scared right, an exhilarated left, and a rookie for a king:

Some of them will spend weeks recovering from the shock of a new dawn. Franco couldn't deal his way out of one last commitment. He bequeathed his people a structure and a pervasive and logical aura of fear—nothing more. Franco probably never intended *La Paz* to extend past his lifetime. It was his peace, his own monogrammed millennial peace.

If you ever have doubts of that, travel to the Basque country, then to Madrid. If there are still doubts, go to the Valley of the Fallen.

Rolling Stone, January 29, 1976

TRIBES

The Eternal City had already smelled like an incinerator for a week. Carlo stuck a plume in his headband, smeared war paint on his face, and walked into the moist tension of the afternoon, once again a Metropolitan Indian—an *Indiano Metropolitano,* an Italian Yippie. He strolled into the rage of March 12—by all accounts the most violent and vicious day in Rome since World War II.

Some 100,000 young Italians were there—many wearing leather jackets bulging with iron pipes and Molotovs and carrying helmets for motorcycles they'd left at home. At strategic points within the huge mass of protesters, kids hugged transistor radios to their ears, all of them tuned to the same underground station, and periodically passed instructions down the lines. When the authorities later tried to close the station, Radio Città Futura, the directors said, "It was a phone-in program. If our listeners call in with reports of police positions and armored car movements during a demonstration, we can't stop them."

Carlo thought the march was beginning peacefully until he saw the kids with the transistors draw the signal of the P-38 out of their

pockets like six-guns from their holsters. This signal, the salute of
the uprisings of 1977, is less subtle than the old clenched fist. You
make your hand look like a gun. Hundreds of people stuck out their
two longest fingers and cocked the other two under their thumbs.
They swung the signals around like karate chops. It spread through
the march. Then Carlo knew it was going to get mean.

Suddenly groups broke off on all sides of the procession, wailing
and dancing into the ancient Roman side streets. They slapped their
puckered lips in bloodcurdling war whoops. Out came the Molotov
cocktails and steel bars, up went the scarves, masks, and goggles.
From tooled leather bags came very new and efficient-looking pistols. The air began to pop.

Carlo joined one of the contingents and bobbed from doorway to
doorway until he reached the Via Giulia, where the shop windows
were already broken and people were looting inside. People were
rushing by with records and tape players. "Proletarian shopping"
was a relatively new aspect of the Italian student movement. He ran
into a gun shop where the owner had locked himself in a storeroom
in the back. Young longhairs were piling rifles, pistols, and ammu-
nition into bags. He ran to another part of the store, grabbed a huge,
white, floating lifesaver with a red flag sticking out of it, and yelled,
"This is what we need! This is what the movement needs! We don't
need that stuff, take these!" He spun around the shop in his war
paint and feathers and tried to tell the others they were taking it all
too seriously.

The élan of several weeks earlier seemed to have turned into desperation. Carlo and the other *Metropolitani* believed that guns were
only necessary to defend the life of the movement. They were going
too far in the gun shop. Some of the heavies laughed at Carlo as he
stood in the doorway with his lifesaver and war paint.

As he started to leave the gun shop, he could see cops dressed
like futuristic gladiators rounding the corner at the end of the street
and firing from behind parked cars. The boy standing next to him in
the doorway began to make little panting sounds, stripped off his
leather jacket, and stuck his arm out in front of him. A bullet had en-

tered near his elbow and left just above the wrist, leaving a slightly larger hole. The boy pushed his glasses to his tearing eyes. He just stood there staring at his arm.

Out in the streets the light was beginning to fade. Cars were burning everywhere; groups of rioters and police curled and dodged through the streets, shooting and then spinning behind walls and ducking into doors and alleyways. When a tear-gas grenade exploded, kids would run into the cover of the smoke, fire, then retreat before the mist had faded.

The battle raged through much of the night: through the piazzas, lit like the infield at a night baseball game by the carbon-arc floodlights on the tops of armored cars, past the stained statues and the beautiful fountains and the churches of the ancient center of Rome. Plainclothes policemen hovered at the edge of the Centro and reportedly beat students on their way home. Demonstrators rampaged through residential areas, knocking on doors and pleading for shelter from charging troops.

The police later reported that twelve cops had been shot on March 12. They called the battle "an urban guerrilla offensive without precedent." The alternative paper, *Rosso,* declared that the "armed violence was carried out by organized groups who left the body of the march, struck selected targets and returned into the group. This military avant-garde," *Rosso* concluded, "was completely accepted by the demonstration because it was an integral part of it."

The minister of the interior warned that "the country may be facing political terrorism with mass student support." The Vatican proclaimed that the violence was yet another facet of "a vast campaign for subverting of traditional values." Giorgio Amendola, one of the Italian Communist party leaders, also condemned the violence and enunciated one of the widely held beliefs as to its cause—that insidious right-wing infiltration was to blame. Amendola said, "We are in Chile before we have even got into government." The prestigious *Corriere della Sera*—the *New York Times* of Italy—said that there was "a presentiment of endemic civil war. . . ."

—

So went the second semester of the year of the counterculture, of the occupation of the universities, and the explosion—the result of ten years during which young people in Italy have been crowded toward the edge of what they believe to be a dead-end society.

Last year there were well over a thousand "politically motivated" major crimes in Italy. Bombs explode every few hours. At least one man breaks out of prison every day. Jail wardens have been arrested for helping right-wing groups and jail wardens have been arrested for helping left-wing groups. You won't find a single person in Italy who doubts that the reason the bombers are never caught is because someone lets them out of jail to plant a bomb, then they come back to prison when they are done, replete with a perfect alibi.

Nearly 100 people have been kidnapped since the beginning of 1976 and over $70 million in ransom has been paid. In February, the first evidence of the long-suspected links between the kidnappings and political violence was discovered when ransom money was found after the arrest of a fascist extremist. Kidnapping is so prevalent that the police now try to freeze the victim's family's assets so that no ransom can be paid. Rich people carry pistols everywhere in chic little leather cases.

Though organized crime has always had political overtones in Italy, a series of recent incidents, including the inadvertent interruption of a Mafia conference in Sicily by two policemen, has shown that there are Mafia people near the top of the ruling Christian Democratic party and Christian Democrats near the top of the Mafia.

The same party and the same men have ruled Italy since the war. Though on average governments have lasted only ten months, the leaders of the Christian Democrats have simply taken turns at being prime minister. Most of them have been implicated or charged with accepting money from either the CIA or from a multinational corporation.

No one believes the official statistics in Italy, but it is safe to estimate that there are around two million young people already unemployed in Italy—some estimates say that there are over three. One million are between 14 and 19 years old. Most of them have high school diplomas and many have college degrees. There are thousands of unemployed lawyers, engineers, and—believe it or not—doctors. All of them are young.

In Europe, unemployment is the most volatile of political issues. When the unemployed are also young and educated, the situation is ripe for chaos, as every dictator knows. Only one man has ever successfully made young people with an education settle for sweeping the streets—and that was Stalin.

In 1962 there were a quarter of a million people in college; there are now around 1.3 million students operating in precisely the same amount of space and with no corresponding increase in the number of teachers. Most corporations stopped accepting diplomas granted after 1968 because they didn't mean anything; this in a country where a university degree is traditionally far more important to a young person's future than in the United States.

Of the more than one million young people who are lucky enough to be registered at a university, only a small fraction have any hope of finding a job. In six or seven years, they've been told, it may open up a bit. So they hang around college as long as possible. The colleges are called "parking lots for the unemployed." The Socialist party leader, Bettino Craxi, calls these students the new, revolutionary "intellectual proletariat."

Just after the first of the year, the universities exploded. They were immediately occupied by people who'd grown up amid what they call the *fantapolitica,* the strategy of tension, or sometimes the "spiral of tragedy"—phrases emblematic of the collective paranoia and desperation that characterized another time in Italy, just before the days of Mussolini.

The colleges became forums for the frustrated, coliseums for the disillusioned. The protest finally burst forth out of the universities in an expression of rage against everything modern Italy has to offer—which isn't much at all. They turned the streets into battlegrounds.

—

"You have to see the campus to believe it," Carlo had said as we passed the gates of the university. It is a lesson in brutality that teaches a lot about Italy.

The University of Rome is supposed to be one of the good things that Benito Mussolini brought to Italy; like making the trains run on time. Mussolini wanted everyone to go to his schools, so he built the university for 20,000 people. Now there are officially 150,000 students, although a recent survey reports that there are 180,000. No amount of graffiti could alter the intractable fascism of those buildings. The white walls adorned by strong mechanistic-looking figures are oppressive in their ugliness. Gutted old automobiles now sit behind the iron gates of the campus and posters and slogans are splattered everywhere. Hundreds of meetings and rallies are announced from the bleached walls. Huge posters charging the man who oversees the police, Interior Minister Francesco Cossiga, with premeditated murder are done in the "Wanted Dead or Alive" motif. Others portray him ominously as General Custer.

It was to this campus that they all came in February. The shooting of a student by a neo-fascist group in one of the classrooms sparked off the occupation of the buildings. All the thousands of Carlos, all of the "thems" in an "us and them" social framework, came to the university to talk about what they were going to do about their lives—all of the students, the unemployed, the freaks from the Campo de' Fiori, the homosexuals, junkies, immigrants from the South who thought they'd find the streets of the North paved with gold, the nostalgic students from the late sixties, revolutionaries (old and new), and even the high school students (who came only long enough to learn the style of the uprising, then returned to take over their high schools). The movement was a coalition of outcasts, heretical Marxists, heretical Catholics, and anyone else who was angry. The newspapers called them the "Immarginati"—the "marginals."

There were the young feminists. Their surging militancy in this most chauvinistic of societies has recently gained tremendous numbers of new recruits. Punitive feminist antirape squads patrol bad areas of some Italian cities and occasionally hunt down rapists privately. Though the various feminist collectives tend to play it down, there are also armed groups of militant feminists who believe that they quite literally have their own battle to fight. The young feminists flocked to the occupied campus and wrote "Hard Times for the Supermale" on the wall and the men visibly paled as they displayed their new hand signal—two fingers moving quickly together like a scissors.

The lecture halls were taken over as places of open assembly. Weeks of leaderless, agendaless, and often surreal discussions ensued. Some political diatribes were heard, but mainly there was a succession of personal testaments. A gay student who'd come down from Milan took the microphone and talked about the nature of his unhappy existence. He was later to say that "it seemed like the only really political thing to do at the moment." In a country in which homosexuality is still closely associated with criminality, people actually showed up in drag.

"I had never talked to more than ten people at the same time in my entire life," Carlo said as we strolled into the back of a political meeting, "and that was to my family. Three weeks ago I addressed several thousand cheering and screaming people. They danced around and gave me joints. They were delirious."

The scene at the university during the winter was anarchic and utopic. People who'd never seen drugs began to consume them and, as the papers gleefully reported, people stayed there at night—in couples. A committee of students asked for certain reforms for their university. They asked for more space, for day-care centers, and for "political control over all exams," which meant that a passing mark was to be guaranteed on all examinations. Parents all over Italy wondered what was happening to their children. "They want to tear down the system," many of them said, and wrote to the newspapers, "but they don't have anything to put in its place." Underground newspapers suddenly appeared proclaiming, "Everything! Now!" A banner was hung outside one of the halls at the Rome campus: "Let us face facts," it said. "We are asking the impossible."

Within this magmatic mutiny there were some very familiar appurtenances: hair to the belt, old-fashioned LSD, and endless raps on Buddhism and various Indian philosophies. The dress, proliferating underground media, music, symbols, and even some of the language were eerily reminiscent of America a decade earlier.

Italian kids all stutter now in vague Italian forms of "like, well ya know, man"—the laid-back new attitudes embedded in the tone. Every other word out of most young people's mouths is *"cazzo,"* a coarse pejorative expletive referring to the male genitalia and a troubling experience if your name happens to be Katz.

Interior Minister Cossiga's name is still plastered all over the walls of Italy. It is spelled "Kossiga" despite the fact that there is no "k" in Italian. Is it the long-lost "k" of "Amerika"? Most people I asked had no idea why it was written with a "k." When I asked Carlo, he said it was the "K" of Kissinger.

It was all different, too. There was no Vietnam War to cathect the energy against a manifest evil. They were reacting against a scattered, messy sort of evil. Universities all over Rome were occupied by people who'd given up trying to figure out who's responsible, who is to be hated or feared.

When we met, Carlo had said, "You're going to feel like you've seen all this before, but don't draw the parallel too far. The economic state of this country makes it all different. Italy is in a state of prerevolution. They'll never buy us off."

Postwar Italy was a capitalist's dream, buoyed by American money, low wages, and high productivity. America arrived in Europe as the ancient Romans arrived in Athens: offering untold wealth while foisting the gifts of an alien culture upon it (computers, Marlboros, and blue jeans). There ensued an "economic miracle" of unprecedented proportions. Between 1950 and 1962, the gross national product of Italy doubled. Streets that were cluttered with bicycles were soon paralyzed by Fiats. Italy was dominated by the dollar and defended by NATO. America brought industrial power and the great corruptive powers that come with it.

The kids on the warpath thus grew up in a world of spanking-new middle-class values that their parents accepted as God's writ. Now there is a generation of "ungrateful kids" who "don't know the meaning of sacrifice." This generation gap is by no means restricted to the middle class. Many of the sons of the Communist party leaders run with the youth movement.

All over Rome, red flags hang from derelict buildings where young people like Carlo live in a variety of communal enclaves. Carlo grew up in one of the ugliest industrial suburbs in Europe. His description of his family sounds more like something out of a working man's *Ozzie and Harriet* episode than from Fellini's memories of an Italian childhood. Carlo's mother says she gave up on him when he quit college and went to live in a commune two years earlier. He says that she is a fat, bitter woman who "feels greater spiritual peace in a new supermarket than in a church." She voted, as have most women in Italy, for the Christian Democrats in every single election and the hulking figure of the church still dictates her fundamental view of the world.

Nearly 10,000 kids run away every year in Italy. One minor vanishes in Rome every week and is never heard from again. That sacrosanct unit of strength and warmth, the Italian family, an institution that increased in strength as a result of traditionally weak governments, is finally falling apart. Carlo never visits his family. They know what he's been up to, but they still send him money every once in a while. Carlo says that his parents' lives are built on work and accumulation and that he will probably never have a chance to work. He says he can't relate to anything about them. He says he loves them.

In all of his 24 years, Carlo had never felt such happiness as he had during his short stint as a Metropolitan Indian. He wants no other description of himself than that he is a child of the movement. "The Indians helped open up the life to millions of people who were ready to deal with the culture," he said. "The Indian experience is a desperate struggle that involves our happiness. It is a war cry."

The Metropolitan Indians were at the center of the uprisings at the universities. In place of a political creed, the *Indiani* believed that the time was right for irony, for laughing at life, for serious cultural vandalism. They reacted directly to the *fantapolitica.* "Irony is revolutionary," they wrote on the walls of the campus. "Fantasy will destroy you," was scrawled over one entire wall of a university building. The Metropolitan Indians demanded unequivocally that all the animals be released from the zoos. It was a militant surrealism. Every time someone got up to speak in the assemblies about the "working class" they got the same treatment. The crowd would erupt into shouts of *"scemo, scemo, scemo"*—fool, fool, fool. At universities and high schools, in front of nuclear power plants, at almost any meeting of any organization, Italian-style Indians began to show up, war dancing into the scene in paint and headdresses. The leaders had names like Crazy Horse and Geronimo. Student meetings and rallies would often degenerate into wild dope-smoking parties, with everyone dancing around the lecture halls Indian-style, singing, *"Hai-yai-yai-yai-yai-yai-yai."*

When the Metropolitan Indians surfaced at the university, the *Time-* and *Newsweek*-style Italian press said that they were a bunch of students who had been reading *Bury My Heart at Wounded Knee.* In fact, the Indians were born outside the university sometime last year. They did local political work in the neighborhoods in Rome and Milan where their communes were located. They gave street parties and tried to gain support for their demands for more open space for the people who lived in their areas. They also took a great deal of LSD. The idea of American Indians came from the local underworld tradition in certain sections of Rome where small-time pistoleros and Mafia types still refer to each other by Indian code names.

Italians are not known for their appreciation of satire, sarcasm, or irony. Even the Nazis felt that Mussolini couldn't take a joke. There are laws in Italy that protect politicians and all public officials from any kind of satirical criticism. Politicians must give their permission before being mimicked on television. Thus, the weapon of the Metropolitan Indians must be respected for what it is. By the time classes started up at the university, the Indians had honed the edges of their knives of sarcasm. The professors were greeted by a 50-foot warning on the wall of the Faculty of Letters building. It said, "A Peal of Laughter Will Bury You."

Most classes began with a few Indians in full gear sitting in the first few rows. Sometimes they'd arrive dressed in bandages with feathers stuck on top. They threw flowers at professors. Twenty *Metropolitani* would burst into a lecture and dance in a circle around the professor, going, "*Ai-yai-yai-yai-yai-yai.*" They'd sing, "You're the stupidest person here. Why do you treat us as such fools?" Nothing could be more brutal for many Italian professors, the most self-important members of the society.

The newspapers called the Indians intellectual terrorists and young people throughout Italy called them wonderful.

Then it got a bit more aggressive as other, more violent students got into the act. Professors were forced to give their lectures on their knees. There were reports of teachers being urinated upon and being "executed" with very real-looking squirt guns. Gay students humped and hugged several white-faced lecturers and people brought their dogs into classrooms to defecate. Students began to demand perfect marks on all their work—or else. In Florence, an entire exam review board was held hostage and were told that they would be thrown out of the window unless they passed everyone on a mathematics test. They did. Several teachers received telephone death threats and others were mugged. It was getting uglier and uglier.

The intensity of the violence built slowly as the movement attracted recruits.

———

One expected result of the proliferating incidents was the further cooperation of Italy's two largest political parties. Throughout the latter days of the spring carnival, after the violence set in, two monoliths—representing the bureaucratic incarnations of ideology and religion—began to gently grind together in the most bizarre of political dances. Leaders of the rival monoliths were at a loss as to the why and wherefore of the violent fury and new antipathy of their children. The Christian Democratic party that has ruled Italy since the war, heirs to a 2,000-year-old religious subculture—a political party whose programmatic commitment to keeping the rival Italian Communist party out of government is not unlike the government of West Germany's strategic relationship to East Germany—began to look for help from that same Italian Communist party.

At the edge of the scene at the campuses stood the unhappy-looking members of the Italian Communist party's student groups, who braved physical attacks to even show their faces on the campuses. A child of the new generation joining the Communist party in 1977 is tantamount to a Berkeley radical going to Harvard Business School in 1967. But the faithful, the young Communist party militants who only months earlier had briefly been campus heroes, continued to come to the university and tried to hawk their newspaper. "How could they do this now," one of them said, "just when the working class is on the threshold of government?"

It is possible to feel sorry for the Communists. They emerged after World War II as the most powerful political force in Italy and were members of the postwar government. Then came the Cold War. While the wartime fascists were rinsed clean, the Communists became the sinister arch enemy who was going to unlock the gates when the vast horde came charging from the East. They were identified with the Soviet Union, the destruction of Western civilization, and with the devil incarnate. They were thrown out of the government in May of 1947 and began a slow process of moving toward power as the party of change.

The party's first substantive electoral gains coincided with the first student uprising in Italy since the war, in 1968. The PCI (Partito Comunista Italiano)—the Peachy, as it is known—was the great red hope for the students in the late sixties and early seventies. The Communists could be trusted; they would purge the corrupt Chris-

tian Democrats; they were smarter, more democratic; they were re-
visionists whose overriding characteristic was humanism. The student leaders of 1968 took off their U.S. Army jackets, shaved their
Guevarist beards, and became functionaries of the party.

During the general elections last year, as every good American
knows, the PCI came within a few percentage points of winning.
Before the elections, the word had gone around to the campuses, the
unemployment organizations, the extraparliamentary groups on the
left, and the shop-floor militants that all of the talk they were about
to hear about a "historic compromise" with the hated Christian
Democrats was just a ploy to gain the power to fundamentally alter
Italian society. The youth flocked to them. Their rallies were like be-
ins and their leaders like pop stars.

Now, Communist party leader Enrico Berlinguer and Christian
Democratic Prime Minister Giulio Andreotti have worked out an ex-
traordinary governing relationship in which the Christian Democrats pass legislation only because the Communist parliamentarians
don't vote. The students call this the government of Berlingotti.
"They are in the Palazzo now," the students say of the Communists
in the corruptive halls of power. They feel hurt and betrayed by the
Communists. Young people hate them and do not consider them a
part of the left. The professors who received the brunt of the abuse
dealt out by people like the Metropolitan Indians were ironically the
Communist professors, known as the Red Barons. The Barons typ-
ify one of the students' main gripes with the Communists: in their
studied paternalism, the professors are men who have a specific and
protected place within a system to which they are in opposition.
Many of the Communist professors brought to their knees were the
radical student leaders in 1968. The students find this to be a fitting
irony.

The Communist youth are a notoriously straight group of young
men and women. Short hair, plain dress, and a mimimum of extrava-
gant extracurricular activity are the mode. "You know we have to see
them shaking hands, too," one of the youth leaders said when I asked
her about the PCI-CD alliance. She went on to confide that there are

small groups within the Communist youth organization that have been affected by the outburst of the counterculture. There have been instances of groups of youth members secretly smoking pot.

The Peachy leaders know that the millions of middle-class Italians who voted for them last year did so, in part, because they figure that the Communists can keep the workers and the youth under control. The party of change and hope has become the party of law and order.

A few weeks into the uprising at the Rome campus the newly responsible party of change decided that the kids had had their fun and that it was time to take things into their own hands:

They sent Luciano Lama, a resistance hero, the leader of the Communist trade unions and one of the most powerful men in Italy, to diffuse the tension of the occupation. Lama is the archetype of the paternalistic, pipe-smoking, Communist godfather/politician. He came into the occupied university and began to talk to around 10,000 milling students and young people from behind a phalanx of PCI "order service" units in their blue outfits. Lama began a heavy liturgic lecture on the virtues of hard work and study. He spoke to a group of people who are guaranteed to be unemployed for what are supposed to be the best years of their lives about "parasites who do not want to work." Many of the parents of the kids in the crowd are members of the Communist party and their children are well aware that Communist trade union protectionism is one of the many reasons that they'll never find jobs. After an hour of listening to Lama's harangue, some Metropolitan Indians went to a wall and wrote, "Put Grass in Lama's Pipe." Other Indians threw flower balls at him while still others got a ladder out of the library and hung him in effigy. Lama's bodyguards were more accustomed to keeping adoring teenyboppers away from their boss than angry students. Pretty soon some rocks came streaming out of the crowd, then some wrenches and iron bars appeared. Suddenly all hell broke loose. Students and order service men bashed each other with pipes and wrenches for half an hour before the police charged the whole crew. Lama snuck out without injury.

Lama later said that it reminded him of "the fascist strong-arm action squads" of another era. The Communist party paper called the incident "antidemocratic provocation . . . animated by a reactionary spirit." The students found this quite funny. People in the streets continued to try to figure out what was going on, and on one of the few remaining unmarked walls at the university, the Metropolitan Indians wrote, "Lamas Belong in Tibet."

The nature of the demonstrations that poured out of the universities all over Italy several times per week after Luciano Lama's expulsion from the Rome campus further terrified a public that has been consistently terrorized for several years. A pattern developed in which the body of a march would move up against the army of riot police, the signal of the P-38 would appear, a shot would be heard . . . then they'd all start shooting. Certain students became adept at treating their fellows' gunshot wounds. By mid-April, this new and frenzied style of demonstration had already claimed several victims. The university continued to be the haven for the counter-culture, the protest, and, increasingly, for the heavies of the "autonomous" groups, the hardliners within the movement, who began to control the assemblies and to map out street action. Though groups like the Metropolitan Indians preferred to fight with sarcasm, the longhairs with the guns were gradually accepted as an integral part of the movement.

—

On April 21, the birthday of Rome, students reoccupied the Rome campus to protest the presence of the police inside the movement's sanctuary at the university. The police proceeded to encircle the four occupied buildings, leaving an opening for the students to get out as they closed the perimeters of the circle. By the time the students had all been chased out of the university buildings, a young police trainee named Settimo Passamonti had been shot in the chest and was dead. The movement had been expecting something like this ever since the death of Francesco Lorusso, a medical student who was shot and killed in Bologna a month earlier. Passamonti became one of nearly 70 Italian policemen killed since the beginning of last year.

Interior Minister Cossiga felt that he finally had the support from both the public and the Communist party to declare war on the movement. He banned all public demonstrations until the end of May and laid down the gauntlet in parliament. He declared that "against those who attack with weapons, the state will react in kind."

At the edge of the huge bloodstain which marked where Passamonti had died, somebody wrote in chalk, "Here lay a cop— Lorusso has been avenged."

"It was on the 21st of April, when Passamonti was killed, that the Indians realized that we had to disperse," Carlo said. He was arranging reams of underground literature in the alternative bookstore that his graphics collective had started. "Things were different at the campus and in the meetings," he said. "We knew that the government's ban on marches was intended to provoke a major confrontation. We told people to go back into their holes like moles. We tried to calm things down. . . ."

When things exploded at the universities, the Metropolitan Indians began to publish daily Dadaesque underground publications with announcements of activities. Now the movement depends on over 100 new underground papers to keep in communication. The material runs from serious alternative bibliographies on housing, drugs, and alternative education, to feminist literature on self-help and R. Crumb–style comix. It is mainly instant journalism written in a wild new code.

The youth movement has also made creative use of the traditionally conservative media institutions. Over 1,000 pirate radio stations have sprung up in Italy during the past two years. There are some 100 stations in Rome alone—some of them operating from balconies in the Hilton Hotel. The most popular and most powerful of the underground stations is Rome's Radio Città Futura.

People at the station readily admit that they were involved in coordinated street action, such as that on March 12. "This radio station is annoying to the powerful," one announcer said. "We are a movement inside the movement."

Radio has always had a potentially powerful political import in Italy. The first voice on Italian radio was that of Mussolini. Città Futura is listened to by hippies, office workers, bank presidents, and can be heard blaring out of Ferraris. It is supported by public subscription and, it is said, by some famous film directors.

I asked one of Carlo's friends at Città Futura if he saw any similarity between the new counterculture in Italy and that of America in the sixties. "I don't really know anything about the American counterculture," he said. "Whatever it was I know it died in 1970."

—

On May 12, the tiny Radical party invited people to defy the government ban on demonstration and to celebrate the anniversary of the Italian divorce referendum victory of 1974 with them in tourist-filled Piazza Navona.

By two o'clock, the Piazza was an ordered mélange of plexiglass riot shields, policemen in chain-mail vests, and endless rows of tear-gas grenade launchers.

Four hours later, tourists huddled in fear near the plaster Berninis in the shops off the Piazza. Outside, young people had built barricades and full-scale guerrilla warfare was in progress. The police had reacted to some jeering and shouts of "*scemi*" by firing their tear-gas grenades against people's heads and backs at close range. Groups of police surrounded anyone who ended up standing alone and beat them senseless. Middle-class liberals who support the American-style, civil-rights-activist Radical party tried to pull policemen off unconscious young people and were beaten to the ground. Shots were popping continually and people were falling wounded. War cries echoed through the tiny streets as the one-sided battle raged toward the river.

A high-school student from the north of Rome named Giorgina Masi could see the havoc from where she stood on the other side of the Garibaldi Bridge. The screams and shots were muffled because the bridge spans the Tiber where the river forks into a whooshing mist. It was quite obvious to the people standing near her that the police had no intention of losing this battle. When her boyfriend turned to her to say something about it, he saw her slumped on the ground with a bullet in her stomach. An hour later, she died.

The bullets on May 12 seemed to be coming from everywhere. It was more chaotic than it had ever been. The next day a photograph published in the Rome daily *Il Messaggero* showed why. The picture clearly showed a hip-looking young man in civilian dress extending a pistol. The paper identified him as a cop.

The Interior Ministry admitted that 30 plainclothesmen had been sent to help the riot squads on that day. Italian riot control has advanced only a bit since the recent days when they'd simply drive their Alfa Romeos through large groups of demonstrators at high speeds. Students had claimed for some time that one major change within the riot force was that it had been inundated with young Serpicos, Starskys and Hutches. On May 12, they were finally proven right.

During the morning of the next day, bombs exploded and blew up parked cars in Rome. A police station in Genoa was bombed, as was a Christian Democratic party office near Florence. Government buildings all over Italy were attacked.

Five thousand students walked slowly to the point on the bridge where Giorgina Masi had been shot the day before. A makeshift tombstone had been set up in the middle of the bridge and hundreds of flowers lay on the pavement near the spot where she had fallen. The monument was guarded by a ring of feminists who sat cross-legged and silent. The student groups stood on one side of the vigil and the police faced off on the other. Once again there was the oppressive tension.

People among the movement crowd began to pull their scarves up onto their faces and many were waving the sign of the P-38. Student marshals managed to move most of the students back off the bridge before the police finally charged. There were only the 15 young women and a little boy left sitting around Giorgina Masi's memorial, so the cops beat them for a while with long bowling-ball-rubber truncheons before destroying the mock tombstone.

The following day the clashes again grew savage. There were battles in Rome, Naples, Milan, and Turin. Firebombs exploded in Bologna, Palermo, and Como. Inevitably, on the third day after Giorgina Masi's death, a 25-year-old policeman was shot and killed during a demonstration in Milan, the fourth cop to be killed in two weeks.

Two days later another haunting photograph appeared in the press of some masked males crouching and firing guns into the demonstration. The faceless figure in the foreground of the photograph held both hands out, one steadying the other. His weight rested easily on his right foot, the left ankle bent inward to balance himself—like a professionally trained marksman. "Finally," the students at the university said, "now we see Cossiga's masked provocateurs in action. No student could learn to shoot like that. . . ."

A few days later, the gunmen in the photograph were arrested: three middle-class high-school students, one age 19, the other two 17 years old. . . .

A few days after the shooting in Milan, the heavies within the movement called a meeting to discuss the violence. It was getting hot in Rome. Outside the university buildings where the meeting was to be held there was a red flag at half mast. On the walls everywhere was written "Giorgina Lives."

Carlo sat stoned in the sun near the entrance to the meeting hall with other Metropolitan Indians. They signaled me over. The Indians had released a statement saying, "We denounce and refute with all of our strength and creativity" the new turn to the violence.

The meeting began, but the Indians stayed outside throwing plastic trash bags full of water on each other. I volunteered to the group that it looked like the violence was completely out of hand.

"The movement needs its own time," Carlo muttered. "You must see that P-38 is an indicator of the violence we have put up with every day of our lives."

"I can't even imagine why someone would bring a gun to a march," I said.

He looked at me with a half smile: "All of this tension and exasperation—call it violence—it must be horrible to you, *compagno,* but it's real. We've talked about the sixties and the days of peace and love. I suppose it is horrible. But you see I can't simply condemn it. I am unable to look at the way things are in this country and accept that the fault is within the movement. And another thing," he said, "if you had a gun and you were Italian you'd bring it to the march."

Inside, a discussion raged as to the role of the *Autonomia Operaia,* the hardcore of the movement. The "workers autonomy" group had come a long way since the days when they dumped garbage on rich people going to the opening of La Scala Opera in Milan. They had become strong within the incubator of the movement. Members of the group claimed that their role was to protect the movement from attacks and provocation from the police. I met some *Autonomia* members who were 15 years old.

The violence surrounding the youth movement was rapidly becoming associated in the public mind with Italy's more premeditating underground revolutionaries—such as the South American-style Red Brigade and the Armed Proletariat Nucleus, organizations that assassinate policemen and magistrates and calmly splinter journalists' kneecaps with bullets.

The movement was becoming criminalized. Metropolitan Indians rarely appeared in war paint anymore; their liberating iconoclasm and infectious smiles seemed out of place now—like lifesavers in a gun shop.

Italy has run out of time, compassion, and money. Everyone knows that something has to happen. The people who are too old or jaundiced or afraid to respond to the tension with overt anger have settled for despair. Nobody thinks it's going to get any better.

The culture continues to twist and turn and spin the excess toward the edge. It is in the throes of a systematic breakdown managed by a corrupted bureaucracy, where a few million angry and idle young people are deciding whether or not to react to the humiliation of their lives by shooting a gun. Europeans now thirst for news in Italy. It is considered to be a nation which reflects an advanced case of a European liberal democracy's current malady. Pundits look at the cascade of factions and at the violence to "decode the anger." One of the Communist professors who has experienced their rage firsthand recently said that the youth are now a separate society on a collision course with everyone else. They have their own culture and their own values. He says they are an institutionalized enemy.

—

One week after Giorgina Masi was killed, Rome was under occupation. "Rome Paralyzed by Fear!" the headlines screamed. Shops and offices were closed, and traffic was lighter than it had been in years.

"The students have finally called for a showdown," people told one another. They had decided to march outside the university in defiance of Cossiga's ban. Everyone knew that a confrontation was coming. Both sides were angry and resolute.

Five thousand of Italy's most highly trained, biggest, and meanest-looking riot troops were deployed throughout the city. Public buildings, party headquarters, and most monuments were ringed by troops. Train stations and airports were full of soldiers looking for trouble. The highways into Rome were lined with tanks and armored vehicles and on all exit ramps from the highway cars were stopped and searched for weapons. Helicopters hovered over everything.

Young people all over Rome turned on Città Futura that morning and heard that plans for the march were off. Cossiga and various union leaders had begged the movement to call it off. While pointing at armored cars and machine guns, they'd pleaded with them. "It's off," Città Futura announced, "go to the university."

By about four o'clock they had arrived at the Rome campus. They milled restlessly in the plaza of the university complex. Small groups huddled around transistor radios and listened to Radio Città Futura begging them to keep cool.

In other parts of Italy there had been ten kidnappings during the week since Giorgina Masi died. Early in the morning of May 19, in

Milan, two bombs had gone off in the subway. In Seveso, just outside of Milan, where poisonous chemicals from a factory have infected thousands of inhabitants and where babies are already being born deformed, three youths had fired bullets into the local health official's legs. In Bologna, unemployed people had raided another unemployment office, and in Genoa, responsibility for an early-morning bombing had been claimed by the Women's Armed Communist Liberation Movement.

By five o'clock, thousands of students and young people were walking in the plaza of the university, walking and talking, milling and flexing their muscles uneasily. Indians and gunmen and 15-year-old feminists scratched and shuffled in the thick dust.

The last man to truly understand the power of this tension was Il Duce himself. Mussolini would never have allowed this aimless milling around. He made them all march instead. He used to make the nuns march. Mussolini loved the tension, he grew strong on the tension. In December of 1933, he described to the Fascist Assembly the three imperatives for rising to the heights of his new dawn: ". . . the third and ultimate, and the most important condition," he told them, "is to live in a period of the highest ideal tension."

The students had composed a telegram to Cossiga: "TO COSSIGA," it said, "THE MINISTER OF THE INTERIOR . . . UNABLE TO ACCEPT HEAD-ON COLLISION AS YOU HAVE SUGGESTED . . . WE CANNOT TAKE RESPONSIBILITY FOR FURTHER BLOODY CLASHES . . . HEAD-ON COLLISION POSTPONED . . . WE ARE INCREASING OUR FRONT FOR THE FINAL SHOWDOWN. . . ."

For six slow hours afterward, well into the night, they milled around the plaza, surrounded by thousands of hot and angry policemen. Some of them looked much too young, others looked very old. Sweating in their faded, too-tight, beltless, red-threaded imitation Levi's and Chicago Cubs T-shirts and khaki army book bags that are big enough for guns, they milled faster and faster. They'd sit on the grass for a minute and then get up for a minute, antsy, itching, and tense. A loud shout would produce a sudden moment of silence. Then the milling would start again.

I walked next to Carlo feeling like an actor in a prison film. We went around to look at the huge piece of graffiti that he had helped paint on the walls during the euphoric days of the occupation. He looked up at it for a second and then walked away, still smiling. In huge letters it said, "WE TAKE BACK OUR LIVES."

By the end of September the harbingers of the new season arose out of the doldrums of the Italian summer. There was more unemployment. Only a week or two into the new academic year one young leftist was killed, a policeman and a civilian shot during demonstrations, and in Bologna and on the campus in Rome, the Metropolitan Indians resurfaced and again took to the war path.

Rolling Stone, November 17, 1977

ETHIOPIA AFTER THE REVOLUTION

The vultures will first peck out your eyes and then tear out your livers.
—ERNEST HEMINGWAY to American journalists, in Ethiopia, 1935

Dogs bark all night in Addis Ababa, a sprawling city which rides high (some 8,000 feet) on the western crest of Ethiopia's central highland. On my first night here I thought I heard gunshots above the yelping of dogs, but the dizzying altitude and sleeplessness from two days of travel left me unsure. At 4 A.M. I walked onto the balcony of the huge, empty Addis Hilton and searched the horizon for the vultures I'd been told had returned to the old land of Sheba after many years to feed off the refuse of revolution.

I was staring into the twilight, watching the colors change on the sides of the mountains, when I heard a strange, cadent sound, a sort of muffled slapping that was soon louder than the incessant barking. After several minutes I went down to the street and stood behind a wall in the receding darkness. I saw columns of young children— most of them under ten years old—being herded through the thin air at gunpoint. They looked straight ahead, hoisting their knees high, as children do when they march, then slapping their bare feet to the pavement in unison. The men leading them shouted commands in Amharic (dominant among the four Semitic languages spoken in Ethiopia), and the children began to run, looking like tall, graceful machines despite their ragged clothes.

I later found out that children all over Ethiopia are kept in prisons at night and then marched through the streets at dawn. They are undergoing "political reeducation" conducted by a four-year-old government that feels their homes lacked the proper atmosphere for them to become good revolutionaries. Residents of Addis reported that the marching had been going on for several months. They said these children were lucky to be involved in "revolutionary training" because it was more than likely their families were already dead.

—

I arrived in Addis on a certain Ethiopian Airlines flight—a condition of my visa, which had been granted suddenly. There were no messages at the hotel, so I called diplomatic contacts who told me that this seemed strange and that I should expect to be contacted and followed if I left my room.

The phone rang once that night. A voice asked, "Are you black?" When I said no, the caller hung up.

At 6 the next morning, a 21-gun salute began the "spontaneous celebration" of Ethiopia's Victory Day. The morning paper promised that "the broad masses of Ethiopia will celebrate the 37th anniversary of victory over the Italian fascists with popular enthusiasm and patriotic sentiment." The streets of the capital were filled with children being gently led toward a full day of "patriotic fervor."

The parade appeared to encompass most colors and all shades of khaki. There were peasant lancers from the countryside and fierce-looking Shoan (a highland province) warriors on short, powerful horses occasionally breaking the long lines of troops, camouflaged jeeps, and thousands of unarmed "urban dwellers" who seemed to be arranged by height. Cripples struggled to maintain formation, wincing in determined denial of pain.

Men, women, and children filed by with rifles slung backward and upside down over their slender shoulders; many of them pressed their palms over the tops of the weapons and stuck their fingers in the hole at the end.

One teenaged soldier asked me to touch his carbine for luck because a "white curse" had been placed on it when he was fighting in the desert. He jabbed the barrel within an inch of my chest and smiled.

A prominent resident of Addis had agreed to meet me at the rally under a tree. The pained lines across the man's forehead told of the difficult changes in his life over the past few years. He said that many of his old friends were dead. "It was always a kids' revolution," he whispered under his breath, watching the chanting crowd, "but look into their eyes now. Look at those faces and see that they no longer believe in anything. If you can't see it now, you will before you leave. Children with guns—it makes me ache. The revolution was supposed to be so much better than this."

—

Forty-three years ago Benito Mussolini drove deep into this mysterious highland kingdom and six years later Ethiopian and Allied forces drove him out again. Victory Day used to be celebrated in early May, on the day Emperor Haile Selassie returned to Addis Ababa from exile in England to reclaim the throne. Ethiopia's new rulers moved the event from a day that marked the return of "the royal family from Bath in England where they lived a pompous and luxurious life" to a day when "the broad masses entered the city."

The abandoned and surprisingly unpretentious royal palace has been empty since the fall of the emperor, Haile Selassie, the Lion of Judah, King of Kings, and Elect of God. The diminutive autocrat had ruled Ethiopia for 57 years, the longest absolutist reign in contemporary history. But by 1973, the world surrounding Haile Selassie's empire had changed so drastically that he'd become a kind of anachronistic figurine who continued to rule the ancient amalgam of kingdoms and sultanates, never doubting the myth of his own invulnerability. He imported prestigious international organizations (the Organization of African Unity headquarters, the United Nations Economic Commission for Africa) to Addis, but ninety percent of the people continued to live in a social system that closely resembled slavery.

During his reign, Selassie not only lorded over Ethiopia but, according to documents produced by his successors, never distinguished between the public treasury and his own, and the entire output of Ethiopia's only gold mine ended up in his Swiss bank vaults.

Of the total arable land in the huge country (equal to the size of Texas, Oklahoma, and New Mexico combined) 65 percent was owned by Selassie, members of his family, or the feudal nobility, and 30 percent by the Ethiopian Orthodox Church, which he held in his fee. One family controlled 6.4 million acres and the 700,000 peasants who worked them. The remaining 5 percent of the land was owned by a small minority of the 33 million Ethiopians.

Nearly half the babies born on Selassie's huge nation-farm died during their first year. The average lifespan was 36 years, partly because there were around three doctors for every million inhabitants. Less than 5 percent of Haile Selassie's subjects could read.

Selassie used to throw bread out the window of his limousine and the children and dogs would fight over it. In one of his last decrees the emperor spent great sums stringing traffic lights through Addis in order—as he'd always promised—to bring Ethiopia into the 20th century. The "old man" never doubted that his people loved him.

In late 1972, two million people were suffering from a famine while Selassie continued to export the paltry quantities of grain and vegetables that the arid land produced. Entire villages perished. Living skeletons crawled from the countryside to the villages and hundreds died in the dust on the main road. When the hardier ones arrived in Addis looking for food, troops set up barricades to keep them away. For six months, Haile Selassie censored reports of the famine because, as he reminded the peasants, these kinds of things had been happening for centuries in Ethiopia and were obviously an edict from God.

Of the more than 200,000 subjects who died during that time, many didn't even know that Ethiopia had a government. After 3,000 years of feudalism, they were only aware of their landlords and the land they could see when the sun was up. Ethiopia was an empire, and the peasantry had never participated in a postwar struggle for independence as had the rest of Africa. For them there were no politics.

For 15 years, Selassie sat on a tiny student movement that opposed his autocratic rule; he made them all write letters of apology when they once mustered the courage to stage a protest march. But when the students at Ethiopia's only university heard about Selassie's cover-up of the famine in February 1973, there were violent demonstrations. The students produced the first political leaflets ever seen in Ethiopia, and their leaders employed the methodology of agitation they'd picked up at Berkeley, Wisconsin, and the Sorbonne. Then all Ethiopia's 17,000 teachers—half of the country's high-school educated stratum—went on strike and brought the country to a standstill. The trade unions called the first successful general strike in the history of independent Africa, and eventually the armed forces joined the uprising. Junior officers threw their commanders into the brig and joined the students in the street. The revolt soon reached the outlying provinces and became a full-blown revolution—not a palace *coup d'état* or a foreign-supported guerrilla invasion, but the most radical revolution since the Bolsheviks.

The army brought down Selassie's cabinet and executed the more powerful among them while the students stood outside the palace and chanted "the fish rots from the head." Thus, in September of 1974, the little 83-year-old man was escorted out of his palace and into a Volkswagen that drove him from the place (as he believed) God had reserved for him in history.

Peasants chased landlords into the forests while people chanted and danced in the streets of the towns. Ethiopians congregated and discussed their future, and women joined them in the daylight, many of them out in public for the first time. A revolutionary generation briefly celebrated, but within two years they would be running for their lives and within three years most of them would be dead.

———

Mengistu Haile Mariam, chairman of Ethiopia's military junta, emerged as the living symbol of the "new dawn." A short, charismatic man, the son of a former slave, he has made himself a more imperial presence than the old emperor himself; his very name—"Mengistu"—when spoken slowly means "the government." Many Ethiopians believe he sleeps in a tank.

Mengistu came to power at the age of 36 by the sheer force of his personality, his brilliant oratorical abilities, and his habit of shooting anyone who got in his way—including the two previous chairmen of the government. He became the leader of an illiterate band of soldiers who, whatever their intentions, were unable to find any of their fellow revolutionaries worthy of sharing the power.

Everyone calls these soldiers the *Dergue*—"the Committee." They operate under the aegis of a coarse, sadistic philosophy they believe is Marxist Leninism—with a vocabulary acceptable to the readers of *Pravda* and a method worthy of the most bloodthirsty French Revolutionary.

"These poor soldiers," the man under the tree said as we listened to different members of the *Dergue* warn that the revolution was being attacked from all sides. "There were 120 of them after the revolution, now there are around 40. They've killed each other off. They've bumped into things they'd never seen or imagined before. They knew nothing of government, of socialism—Cubans and Russians—and to this day still don't. One in a hundred of them has even read Marx. They tried taking lessons in Marxism at 6 in the morning at the beginning. You got a sense that right after the revolt they really wanted to do something good."

Toward the middle of last year, Mengistu pulled out all the stops. "It is an historical obligation," he said then, "to clean up vigilantly using the revolutionary sword." He announced that the shooting was about to start and that anyone in the middle would be caught in the cross fire. In what came to be known as the "Red Terror," he proceeded to round up all those who opposed the military regime. According to Amnesty International, the *Dergue* killed over 10,000 people by the end of the year. One antigovernment party, mostly made up of students and teachers, was singled out as "the opposition."

The Red Terror operated quietly and efficiently under the media cover provided by a vicious desert war that started when Somalia invaded eastern Ethiopia ten months ago. Around this time President Carter abandoned a long-term military agreement with Ethiopia on the stated grounds of "gross and systematic human rights violations" and Cuban soldiers and Russian arms poured in to protect and "consolidate the gains" of the revolution.

By the time the Somalis were finally chased from Ethiopia's eastern front two weeks before I arrived, the politics of the revolution had been further obscured by Mengistu's determination to fight yet another war against secessionists in the country's northern province of Eritrea.

After months of killing Ethiopian youth along with assorted Somalis and Eritreans, Mengistu declared to the world that the "antipeople forces who had lined us up for their lunch—we have had them for breakfast."

—

A belt fastened while running will become undone
while running.
—old Ethiopian proverb

There are jails all over Addis. The number of political prisoners in a given jail can be estimated by the number of women who wait outside at lunch time. It is an Ethiopian tradition for a prisoner's family to take responsibility for sustaining him. If a whole family is in prison, then friends must help by bringing food. Sometimes families arrived at a prison and were handed a bundle of clothing and told not to return. There are around 320 prisons in Addis alone, with capacities between 20 and several thousand. They are all filled.

The French daily *Le Monde* estimated recently that there are well over 100,000 political prisoners in Ethiopia. They are all people who have been associated with opposition to the regime and thus accused of being members of the underground Ethiopian People's Revolutionary Party—the EPRP—an organization made up largely of the students and teachers who brought down the emperor.

A few days before I arrived in Addis, the Red Terror campaign had been briefly stepped up after a four-week lull. The Red Terror had become more discreet since the open street battles. But discretion meant only that there were fewer bodies of young people left on the streets in the morning. The bodies were often adorned with signs that noted revolutionary crimes: "This is for revenge" or "The Red Terror will triumph," or sometimes, "This killing was the result of mistaken identity."

———

I met a middle-aged worker during my first week in Addis who spoke impeccable English. He agreed to show me around. I warned him that I might be followed, but he just smiled. His attitude toward me seemed to vacillate between camaraderie and contempt. When we'd pass a particularly ravaged beggar he'd stare at me for a reaction then snort through his nose and shake his head. One time he pointed to a young man being led away at gunpoint and said, "Welcome to Africa, brother."

Addis Ababa is a bizarre city. There is no centralized slum. From the air it looks a bit like Miami, but if you look closely you see that each villa, embassy, bank, office building, or ministry is ringed by unparalleled squalor. There are green patches of scrub throughout this capital where oxen and cows led by ragged tenders graze and occasionally laze through the streets. Just before I arrived in Addis, the government lifted its unspoken ban on public mourning dress and the streets were full of women dressed in black.

We walked to the old market district, the largest open market in Africa, and strolled amid the spice stands and colorful cloth. A few years ago you could buy hand grenades in this *mercado*. It is now considered EPRP territory and has recently been the scene of many shootings.

Each time we crossed one of the wider roads, my companion would say, "Now we are in Higher 12, Kebele 16," or, "This is Higher 2, Kebele 12." Ethiopia has been subdivided into 2,000-to-3,000-person units. In the cities, the units are called *kebeles* (pronounced "keh-bellies"). The term refers to both the new well-demarcated geographical areas of a city and the organizational association that is supposed to be democratically run by elected officials. There are 289 *kebeles* in Addis. The *kebele* associations serve as city hall, district court, and local place of business. Literacy campaigns, hygienic programs, and communal shop systems are all run out of the *kebele*. All members of a *kebele* receive intensive political indoctrination through the cadres in the organization.

As with so many other accoutrements of the revolution, however, something happened at the *kebeles*. Each house in a *kebele* district has a number on it and strict tabs are kept on movements—day and night. If anyone sleeps over at your house or you are out for a night—the *kebele* must know. Absences from official demonstrations and community activities are carefully noted. Each *kebele* has a defense squad whose job it is to protect the revolution. They patrol the streets of their district at night and have pledged to shoot people out after the midnight curfew.

Last year, when Mengistu put the revolution "on the offensive," the *kebeles* became the *Dergue*'s instrument of the Red Terror. The young toughs of the *kebele* defense squads were issued rifles and told to kill for the revolution. Group executions continued every night through the spring of last year. Those who said the wrong things at *kebele* political meetings were sometimes shot in the back of the head before they finished their sentences.

Telephone numbers were publicized so that citizens could turn people in secretly. Children informed on their parents. The young defense squad members killed people over girlfriends and for simple revenge. The power within each *kebele* shifted to its most bitter and violent members. People who had never exercised power or control over anything were suddenly given guns.

The killing became so arbitrary and indiscreet that the *Dergue* recently ordered the *kebeles* to be less blatant. When some of the more active *kebeles* in Addis wouldn't stop the open exterminations, the *Dergue* decided to make an example of six *kebele* chairmen. They were hung last year in a public ceremony replete with spectators.

"A few months ago," my guide said as we stood outside the gate of his own *kebele* before a meeting one evening, "they decided they wanted confessions. The *kebele* would assemble and a man would get up and explain that he had a list of EPRP operatives and sympathizers in his hand and that everyone had to confess. For those who did not confess and make a public exposure, the revolutionary justice would be more severe. You can imagine—people were turning themselves in everywhere.

"Some of the confessions are so emotional now that everyone cries. A man stood up a few days ago and confessed to being an EPRP hitman who had killed 24 people—including several of my friends. He was a former secretary of the teachers' union. He went for rehabilitation and is learning to defend the revolution. . . ."

He kept looking at me for my reaction. "I'll tell you another thing that is just beginning," he said. "I've seen people announce to the *kebele* that they cannot change their belief, that the *Dergue* is fascist and should come down. They *ask* for revolutionary justice. So the bodies that end up on the street these days are no surprise to anyone. For most people now this revolution is about survival, not commitment."

On more than one occasion, I was told the tragic story of Mr. Henno Kiffle as an example of the state of the *kebele* system and a sort of parable for the revolution. Henno was a young man whose uncle was a member of Haile Selassie's inner circle. Thus Henno worked hard to be a good *kebele* member to assure people of his loyalty. He was eventually asked to run for *kebele* office. He immediately received letters from the EPRP underground warning him that if he ran for a post they would kill him, but when he then told the *kebele* he would rather not run they questioned his loyalty. Despite several subsequent beatings by EPRP men, he ran and was elected to office and later became the *kebele* chairman. He ran his end of the Red Terror with zeal. One night he went so far as to kill nine "counterrevolutionaries" and gouge out their eyes. Then Henno was executed by a higher *kebele* authority. The nature of the crimes that led to his death had nothing to do with his overzealous defense of the revolution—he was killed for having proven ties to the Selassie regime.

After several days in Addis, I became preoccupied with the question of why the *Dergue* had wanted me to see the "gains of the Ethiopian revolution." The thought of accounting for myself had me scared. I decided to check in with the Provisional Military Government of Socialist Ethiopia and find out what was going on.

I was searched and led past the armed guards into the lobby of the modern foreign ministry building located across the street from the hotel. As I was looking around for the right office, I noticed a long series of posters adorning one wall. There were numerous dark squares spread across sheets of paper in an orthogonal pattern. As I walked up to the posters I realized that there were hundreds of small photographs of young men and women arranged over the surface of the posters.

"I think we got most of them," a man standing next to me mumbled, then proceeded to explain that the wall represented a giant wanted poster.

"What happened to them?" I asked.

"Revolutionary justice," he said and drew his hand across his neck.

"I thought they were photos from a college yearbook," I said.

"Yes," he replied as he walked toward the staircase, "I think they are."

—

The Addis Hilton, the Comrade Hilton, sits on a hill overlooking the old imperial palace. The hotel was built to coincide with Ethiopia's entrance into the 20th century as a tourists' paradise. It still boasts a staff of over 200 even though there are few guests. The *Dergue* gives the Hilton some business by holding meetings there, despite the fact that they consider the Hilton the source of most rumors and much decadence. A Muzak version of "Power to the People" echoes through the halls at all hours. Among the few paying guests were two or three Dutch and German businessmen and their bevy of teenaged hookers, the foreign minister of the *Polisario,* the revolutionary guerrilla group working out of the Western Sahara, and an American AID worker who was due to be shipped to Indonesia in six days. The American refused to leave the hotel, saying that he'd "made it this far" and "wasn't about to risk it all now."

"It's the French Revolution out there," he declared one day from the chair in the lobby he never seemed to leave. "Lenin would roll over if he saw this: it's the goddamned French Revolution."

One night toward the end of my stay a famous reporter called from his room and asked to "shoot the breeze." I told him about the upheaval I'd been observing, and he gave me a lecture on the principles of "journalistic cooperation" and kept insisting that he could be of great help if I'd convince my skittish contacts to talk, but none would agree.

He later went on a short, government-controlled visit to a *kebele* and had conversations with diplomats, engineers, veterinarians, and various other wealthy Ethiopians. His observations later appeared in the *New Yorker.*

The Germans at the hotel ordered their women around unmercifully, continually announcing to the others at the pool that they would take the girls "back upstairs" if they didn't openly contend that Germans are better in bed than Ethiopians—something the women refused to do.

The hotel guests were usually joined at the pool by some of the fellow-traveler expatriates in Addis who have come to live near an honest-to-god revolution. There were some European flyboys, former Air America gunrunners, and spray pilots, among a host of other tradesmen, war jockeys, and latter-day sutlers who hang on the edges of brushfire wars and revolutions.

The second-rate colonial scene was supplemented by the arrival of French women in bikinis—most of them teachers or wives of diplomats—who endeavored to make even the most turbulent hellhole appear as a scene out of *Emmanuelle.*

—

You need a pass to leave Addis and, as I didn't even have one to *stay* there, I was hesitant to apply. However, due to some fortuitous assistance and the fact that I was able to duck down behind the seat of the jeep at the checkpoint, I headed south out of the city one glorious day into the hay-colored countryside of the great Abyssinian highlands.

People were being herded along the road at gunpoint everywhere we went. They were poorer and more primitive the further we traveled from Addis. We began to roam the countryside in search of the great lost virtue of the motherland's revolution or at least some Cuban soldiers, who tend to keep away from the cities. We searched by day and at night sat around killing mosquitoes the size of horseflies with a copy of Evelyn Waugh's *Scoop* (the sarcastic—if not racist—novel published in the thirties that includes vivid descriptions of white journalists covering a war in Abyssinia) and watching spiders the size of birds. An American mercenary, an old Africa hand, once told me that in Ethiopia there is a spider that eats only living flesh. It's called the camel spider and is equipped with a prong on its back that emits a local anesthetic. He told me that at night the camel spider descends while you sleep, gives you a shot, and eats your lips. I slept with my hand over my mouth.

—

I was staring into a big brown lagoon near Langano, around 200 miles south of Addis, when I was surrounded by 15 peasants with rifles. A small man wearing robes and holding a sten gun approached me and pinned a paper badge on my shirt. "What are you doing here?" he asked.

"Visiting," I answered.

"You must be a Communist then," he said.

"Of course," I replied nervously and there were smiles all around. "We are revolutionary guerrilla fighters, the defense squad of our peasants' association," the man continued. "We want you to help us."

In March of 1975, the *Dergue* proclaimed a transformation that was more radical than anything in China, Cuba, or Vietnam. It dispossessed all landlords, nationalized Ethiopia's 457,256 square miles, and then redistributed the land to the people. The act electrified the peasants and confronted them with a concept of politics and radical change they never could have imagined. So the *Dergue* closed the high schools and the university and sent the students and teachers to the countryside to explain it to them. They called it the *zemacha;* 60,000 students and teachers operated like a radical peace corps—some 3,000 of them died at the beginning, often because they refused to go and sometimes because the peasants they went to teach were less than receptive. When the students left, the Ethiopian provinces were subdivided into 27,000 small units that parallel the *kebeles* in Addis.

As we walked down the beach one of the peasants told me about the counterrevolutionary they'd killed the night before and another showed off his new Russian-made Kalashnikov assault rifle. He cradled the weapon lovingly, then shouldered it with a snap and a smile.

The defense squad wanted to nationalize a motorboat that was sitting on the beach. It belonged to a bald Englishman I'd run into earlier that day. We had had a short unpleasant conversation. "I've been vacationing in Ethiopia for years," the man had said, "and I'm not about to stop because of some revolution."

"You really must love the country," I said.

"I do," he sniffed, "except for all the *blacks.*"

The peasants asked me if I could figure out how fast the boat could go. I told them I thought it was quite fast.

"It isn't," the Englishman whined, "besides, it's mine."

"You're in Ethiopia," one of the men said proudly. "There is no private property." They all smiled and nodded in agreement.

I suggested that the boat was fast enough but that it was rather small for all of them. They agreed and decided to set off on foot. I asked the young man with the sten gun what it was like for him before the revolution. "Before the revolution," he said, "I would have called that white man 'master.' "

While I was in Ethiopia there was increasing evidence of friction between the provincial socialist units and the *Dergue* in Addis. There had been two major call-ups of peasants to join the mammoth people's militia in the wars in Eritrea and the Ogaden Desert. A third call-up had recently been announced, but after observing that no one had returned from the wars, many of the peasants refused to go.

On the way back to Addis we encountered the largest military convoy I've ever seen, made up of the men who taught the peasant militia how to fight, the men whom Brzezinski refers to as "the surrogates." Near the Debre Zeyt air base, with its parking lot filled with gleaming MiGs, the road was filled with Cuban troops escorting looming cannons, multiple rocket launchers, and electrical generators the size of houses down the thin road. The Cubans stood near the road looking almost chic in their cowboy hats, green T-shirts, and baggy pants. They acted weary but friendly. Some peasants had told me that at night the Cubans sing sad Spanish songs which the Ethiopians had taken to be religious, or mystical. They seemed to understand the Cubans' songs about as well as they understood their magical weapons. To people who previously considered a strong stick a formidable offensive tool, the Cubans' Russian-made weaponry may as well have been death rays.

Members of the 40,000-man Ethiopian regular army seem proud that they have never fought directly with the Cubans. The American-trained regular Ethiopian troops contend that they are offended by the Cubans' rowdy battle style. The regulars think the Cubans are well suited to training and fighting alongside the peasants—which is probably true and is probably why the Cubans' battle record on foreign excursions is so much better than ours.

Immediately after the battles for the Ogaden cities of Harar and Dire Dawa there were pictures of locals kissing Cubans as they climbed down from their tanks. But by the time I got to Ethiopia there were rumors of Cubans raping Ethiopian women and disrupting *kebele* authority.

I asked a man in a jeep why he fought another country's battle. He looked at me with exasperation. "Because, *comrado,*" he said, "I am a revolutionary."

—

Eritrea, the northernmost province, has been in a state of open insurrection since it became part of Ethiopia in 1962. Mengistu has vowed to crush the powerful secessionist armies that control 90 percent of the region and nearly 100 percent of the public support (largely as a result of the atrocities committed on civilians by Mengistu's troops in the region).

Eritrea provides Ethiopia's sole access to the sea; without it, the country is reduced to a vast, underdeveloped landlocked state. Mengistu considers the Eritrean rebel forces to be "separatist bandits" and announced from Cuba as I was leaving Ethiopia that as he takes on the guerrillas "the Cuban masses will be with us."

Mengistu has pursued the Eritrean war more ruthlessly than Selassie ever did. He has ordered two quixotic if not suicidal peasant marches into the region since taking power. In both cases his troops were cut to pieces by the determined hill-based guerrillas. When his army scattered, he had the commanding officer shot. South Yemeni pilots in Russian MiGs spotted by Cuban ground troops have been dropping Israeli napalm and bombs on the guerrillas for weeks with no discernible results.

Cuban diplomats clearly imply that they don't want to fight Mengistu's battle there. The Cubans were friendly to the Eritreans; they trained their guerrilla leaders in Cuba in 1969 and '70 and eye-witnesses say the liberation forces still paste Fidel Castro's picture on the inside of their tanks.

"The Eritreans are just like you," I said to one of the Cuban soldiers, "how can you kill them?"

"I hope I don't," he said.

A few days after I left Addis the Cuban ambassador and his friendly first secretary, Frank Ortiz, attempted to insist that the *Dergue,* among other things, begin to negotiate a political settlement in Eritrea. Both men were expelled.

The Eritrean rebels are among the toughest, most fanatical fighters in the world. Old Italian soldiers still tell stories of tribal warriors who fought alongside the Eritreans wearing their enemy's genitalia around their necks as souvenirs.

"Let the Cubans and Russians come and fight in Eritrea," said one Eritrean spokesman, "for it will be their Vietnam."

—

Beware Imperialism Is Not Dead Yet
—banner near Addis' Revolution Square

Professor Korovan, late of Moscow State University, rose to the sound of a collectivist sigh. Over 100 Addis University students waited for him to fluff his gray hair and straighten his gray sport coat and tie, before he began to read from an article about capitalism written by Frederick Engels. The students kept turning to each other in disgust during the reading, asking their friends what in the world Korovan was saying. The professor paused occasionally to search, with a meaningful look on his face, for the right English word—it was usually "emerge." He went on to speak of the "natural laws of ee-oh-lay-shun." One of the students said, "What?" and then others started in, and finally the whole class was saying, "What! What! What!" less as a question than a protest, like inmates banging their cups in a prison film.

"You all know theese word," Korovan said. "You all know it— ee-oh-lay-shun."

"No," they chanted. "No. What. No."

Korovan turned to the blackboard, "Ee-oh-lay-shun," he barked, then he wrote the word "volition" on the board.

The Soviets are not unaware of the language problems the Russian professors who have virtually taken over Addis University are encountering. They have even suggested a remedy for the situation—that Russian be taught to all Ethiopian children in secondary school.

Before sitting in on Dr. Korovan's class in Marxism, I'd gone to see the vice-president of the university to extend regards from an American professor who once taught there. When the man heard that I was a journalist he seemed delighted. "You see," he said, "Ethiopia is not a closed society after all." He said that he was hurt that American academics had not given proper support to the continuing revolution. "Sure, we've made big mistakes, but our friends haven't come to our aid. Where are the people who sympathized with us under Haile Selassie? As soon as the Russians are involved we are forgotten." As I left his office he assured me that the campus was now safe. "The university," he declared, "is now stabilized."

Two waves of student executions took several hundred lives this year. So the students have adopted a look of studied lethargy that they hope will keep them alive. "It's fairly clear that two-thirds of the students were against the *Dergue*," one of the students later ventured, "one-third supported them. Of that original two-thirds against them—I'd say half are dead."

Since Korovan's lecture of the day had concerned the class conflict that occurs at the heights of capitalism, I later asked him if Ethiopia hadn't experienced a mighty short bout with capitalism to have reached its highest stage. He smirked and suggested that I didn't know what I was talking about. I then asked him what he likes about Ethiopia.

"I must admit I'm a romantic about it; you know, I missed my revolution." His eyes drifted up to a portrait of Lenin that hung over his desk. "I'd only known about revolution from books, but here— *here,* I've seen something here."

The Russians make much rhetorical use of the "obvious parallels" between the Ethiopian and Bolshevik revolutions. I asked Dr. Korovan to be specific. He thought for a minute, then raised one finger. "The Red Terror," he said, "there's something."

———

Ethiopians say the Russians have contributed to the rise in prices and believe they have "stolen" Ethiopia's coffee crop for years to come in exchange for arms. They are called the Ethiopian word for selfish—one of the worst qualities a human being can have in this culture. "Watch them ignore the beggars," one woman suggested, "or watch them buy like children in the stores. They buy everything—all their clothes are new."

Mengistu himself is said to mistrust the Soviets. He has apparently never forgiven them for telling him to move the Third Armored Division away from the Ogaden Desert to the Sudanese border in March 1977, a move which precipitated an invasion by the Somali army that threatened Ethiopia's existence.

After the Somalis invaded, the Russians made amends for their bad advice to Mengistu by planning a counteroffensive. Those who witnessed the Ogaden campaign say that the Russians were out for more than victory. They contend that Mengistu was told to move his division away from the Somali border only after a meeting in Aden in early March of last year. Somali leader Siad Barre had apparently promised not to attack Ethiopia in front of Nikolai Podgorny and Fidel Castro—and you don't break promises made among those kinds of comrades. The Russians airlifted nearly $1 billion worth of weapons. Troops and tanks were dropped behind Somali lines and the final artillery assault on the Somali stronghold at Jijiga has been compared to Marshal Zhukov's attack on Berlin at the end of World War II—during which the general is said to have read his *Pravda* by the light of artillery explosions for several days.

"I think the Russians are going to regret this commitment very soon," a longtime observer noted. "This country has a history of great suspicion of foreigners of all descriptions. Foreigners in Ethiopia usually get their asses kicked."

—

> The future of revolutionary Ethiopia is in the hands of its
> sons and daughters
> —banner headline from the Ethiopian *Herald*

At the age of twenty-four, Adano considers himself a survivor of his generation. When it was safe to talk, I asked him how many of his friends were dead from political violence. He counted his fingers twice before looking up. "There's only one left now. One of my best friends from school even worked for a *kebele* on the other side from us. One night an EP unit killed him, so it comes from all sides."

The hunted members of the underground proved surprisingly accessible. I had stood in the shadow of the bread line as I'd been told and was ready when the young man with primal Amharic good looks and bell-bottom blue jeans approached me and asked me to follow him at a distance and not to speak.

We began to travel through parts of Addis I hadn't seen. We went into buses and out the back; through churches and into sewage gullies. We strolled through a muddy depression lined with shanty huts, where a swarm of partially clad children streamed out of the dwellings and surrounded me, reaching with obvious fascination toward my conspicuous red hair. They were shouting *"faranj! faranj!"*—"foreigner foreigner."

Past the row of huts, the fellow turned to me nervously, "So you want to know about the party?"

"Are you in the EPRP?" I asked.

He gasped at the initials. "Please don't say that; don't say that again. Please whisper," he said.

Adano had just been released from prison after six months of reeducation. "I got off with some beatings, but others were tortured. They whipped people with metal cables, poured hot oil in their ears, and even stuck hot wires through people's hands." There were other reports in Addis and by Amnesty International that people are chained to poles and left to die in the sun and that hot iron bars have been inserted in young girls' vaginas.

The raging power of the *kebeles* during the Red Terror had made life in the underground impossible, so public confession and subsequent political "reeducation" had become a key to staying alive for people like Adano. You just memorize the right slogans and hope that you never slip. Adano emerged from prison having signed a pledge of loyalty to the revolution and carrying both a certificate attesting to his rehabilitation and a warning that his next mistake will be his last.

He spoke with pride of the 25-year-old member of the EPRP's Central Committee who had avoided capture by jumping to his death from a building two days earlier. The *Dergue* has been unable to capture any of the underground leaders of the EPRP.

Things had changed considerably since the disillusioned students and teachers returned from their "*semacha*" in the countryside to challenge the military regime—usually by joining the EPRP, the underground party of the opposition and, they insist, the first party of any sort in Ethiopia's history.

When they'd first returned to the cities they'd led innumerable marches and students used to give lectures in bars and raise critical placards at public events. But last year, the EPRP and the *Dergue* went to war. It's not clear if the EPRP's "white terror" preceded the *Dergue*'s Red Terror. The EPRP did demand that power pass to the civilian party and the *Dergue* did say no. The EPRP had beaten people who supported the *Dergue,* bombed installations, and assassinated some of the *Dergue*'s functionaries. The *Dergue* fought back through the *kebeles* and massacred at random. Every day the Ethiopian *Herald* boasts that "the Red Terror Continues to Bear Fruit," listing more deaths of "the antipeople forces of the so-called EPRP." They publish photographs of captured EPRP weapons; one showed a table full of typewriters.

Adano says he drinks now to muster the courage to continue. "If you get drunk enough, you don't choke," he explained. "And if you are picked up you have cover from your drunkenness. Many of the drunks and beggars on the streets of Addis at night are ours.

"I am in the communications section. I take messages through the city and distribute our information. The EPRP is broken into five units: mine, the women's group, two organizational recruiting wings, and the military unit."

He contended that certain strategic information the EPRP obtains comes from sources near or in the *Dergue* itself and that arms come to them easily from Somalia, despite the *kebele*'s almost daily house-to-house searches for guns.

His mission the night before had been to write, "The time is now for a government of the people" on a wall, but some trouble with license plates had caused him to fail.

He seemed unsure of his mettle and kept asking me if I thought he was a brave man. He seemed genuinely ashamed when he told me he'd never killed one of the "fascist enemy." "But I know this city," he said, "I know where they look and where they don't. I could take you with us—a white man like you—for days and they'd never know what was going on. I'm a warrior." It seemed that all the death he'd seen had left him feeling guilty—at the age of 24—for being alive.

We continued through the city. He signaled to me at intervals and told me not to talk and even left me at one point and rejoined me in a different part of town.

We passed the large red palace that houses *Dergue* and I said something and pointed up at the wall.

"Don't," he hissed, "don't point, don't even look." He was scared.

We walked into the old lion zoo and watched a cheetah stalk his shadow in his tiny cage. Adano spoke in a resonant whisper, stopping when a guard passed nearby. He wanted to know where I went to college and asked if I'd ever heard of the University of Michigan where some EPRP colleagues had gone to school. He kept staring at the cheetah. "They're dead now."

Adano went on to tell numerous tales of the *Dergue*'s activities. Based on his information I was later able to confirm that there are at least two rural concentration camps in Ethiopia with 4,000 to 5,000 detainees each. Reports indicate that the death rate is up to several hundred a day from dysentery. The people in the camp are largely students.

"It was really fantastic at first," he said after a long silence. "There was this solidarity. I saw the change when I came back from the south where I'd worked with the peasants. I still have my contacts there. The peasants understand the EPRP; they know we can't have a military dictatorship in Ethiopia.

"We used to have these meetings in Teglammon Square. We had big plans. . . ."

I asked him how he describes himself politically.

"I'm a democrat," he answered.

—

I had already made plans to see Adano the next afternoon when the foreign ministry asked me to come to a meeting that was billed as a political inquisition. I made a reservation to leave Addis the day after the meeting and tried not to consider the possibility that they knew of my EPRP guided tour of Addis.

I had identified myself to the Ethiopian authorities several days earlier in order to ask for an interview with Chairman Lieutenant Colonel Comrade Mengistu. I submitted written questions that a man at the Ministry of Information and National Guidance considered inappropriate—especially, for some reason, the one in which I asked Mengistu if his military training in Savannah, Georgia, had helped prepare him to lead the nation.

I was seated in a room at the Foreign Ministry with five young men in dark suits. Two were from the Foreign Ministry, one was from the Ministry of Information, and one represented the mysterious Ethiopian Revolutionary Information Committee—known as ERIC.

The men began asking me about the political nature of *Rolling Stone* and admitted that it had been the subject of some debate.

I'd heard of the man from ERIC and began asking him questions about the American roots of the split between the EPRP and the original pro-*Dergue* students. I'd been told that the man had been president of one of the factions when he studied in the States. We talked about an EPRP fund-raising event he had attended at Columbia University in 1975. He seemed uncomfortable discussing the days before classroom arguments turned into killing.

Until this year the government and antigovernment students and intellectuals were roughly divided by the source of their foreign education. The leaders of the EPRP are (were) mostly American educated and the leaders of the group called the *Meisone* are (were) mostly European-educated Marxists. The *Meisone* supplied the *Dergue* with ideology and advice for some time. The *kebele* system was largely their idea, as was, according to some accounts, the Red Terror. It is said that they turned their backs on most of their former classmates in favor of the *Dergue* so they could play the role of the Bolsheviks with them when the time was right. But Mengistu had other plans for his erstwhile tutors. Under the cover of the Somali war most of them were imprisoned or killed.

One of the men said, "Who is this Joseph Kraft?" referring to the well-known reporter who was staying at the Hilton. "He keeps demanding a car and driver and we've never heard of him."

"He's famous," I said. "He was a friend of John F. Kennedy's." The man who asked the question rolled his eyes.

I was asked during the meeting if I would stay in Ethiopia another week for an official tour. I then admitted that I'd seen the countryside already and felt that I had a strong sense of the gains of the revolution. One of the men laughed, the others didn't.

I lied openly when they asked me my impressions of the revolution, all the while flashing on the variety of faces I'd seen, from the man who'd shown me his *kebele* to the peasants at the lake; from the soldiers to the prominent man who had prophesied that I would "see what the revolution can mean in terms of the sacrifices borne by the common man"; and I repeatedly focused on Adano, with his studied look, dispassionate yet despairing; with his bent dialectic and belief in variations of white men's ideas from the last century. . . .

H. L. Mencken once wrote that any journalist who rates "spats and a walking stick" should cover at least one revolution and one lynching. Somehow I'd missed the part of the Ethiopian revolution that featured the only activist students to come out of the sixties and successfully change a society—and had arrived in time for a modern variation on their lynchings. I'd also felt the cheapness in the air long enough to have been altered by it. I thought about Adano and realized I'd lost touch with the idea of risk as I continued to fabricate and taunt in the government office. There was this nagging bitterness attending my frustration: that covering the backside of Third World revolutions had become a process of evaluating relative levels of horror rather than chronicling increments of human liberation.

The revolution in Ethiopia had begun in order to allow people who had never been free to partake of those endeavors which have come to be considered part of being a human being in the modern world. It vowed at the beginning to establish a "completely free society devoid of exploitation, oppression, injustice, and differences based on religion, tribe or sex."

Mengistu has argued that despite everything the only "objective" way to look at Ethiopia today is in comparison "with past injustices and oppression." It is significant that the peasants I saw plowing the light, cracked dirt with long sticks or walking ten miles across a plain to fill a small gourd with water still live only if they never stop working—but now they do it for themselves.

Yet, I kept thinking about the term *ishi gitaye,* words I learned in Addis that mean "yes master." It died out for a while after the uprising but has lately reappeared in conversations between Ethiopians and their *kebele* chairmen.

What the *Dergue* has done to its children—wiping out the only generation that could have run Ethiopia with skill or vision through the end of this century—reaches a level of masochism that is defined by totalitarian ferocity, unprincipled and insane.

"Mr. Katz," one of the men finally said at the end of the meeting, "we're sorry but this was a mistake. There are certain times that are more conducive than others to have observers at a revolution—and this is not a particularly good time."

I stood up and told them I had one more request. I wanted to know why my visa had been granted.

"We don't know," one of them said.

"Then can you tell me who authorized it?"

"We're looking for that person," the man at the door said as he opened it wide.

—

> There was reason to fear that the revolution, like Saturn,
> might devour in turn each of its children.
>
> —LAMARTINE

After an involved series of messages, I again made contact with Adano. He seemed genuinely glad to see me but agreed that I should leave after hearing of my meeting with the government representatives.

We walked through Addis until dusk, talking about what had happened in Ethiopia. We discussed the work of the great Ethiopian writer Daniachew Worku, the poet of the generational divide. "It had a lot to do with the war between the ancients and moderns," Adano said, "and a lot to do with the problems of fathers and sons. Daniachew understood it."

Adano was born in a rocky place near Menx in the north. "You need a mule to get there. My father is a peasant who tries to farm in rock. He doesn't understand very much." He shook his head. He'd once tried to get out of Addis and go back home but his *kebele* wouldn't allow him to leave. They are afraid that young people who leave Addis will return to the scene of their *zemacha* to incite the peasantry.

"I was going to be a pharmacologist. You have them in America?"

I nodded.

After he gave me directions, we parted in a northern section of the city. "Write a good article about what has happened," he said, "about those stupid people with their guns. . . ." Then the late sun broke across his face and I saw that he was beginning to cry. And more than the guns or even the fear, I still remember the look on his face. "I'm weeping," he said, blinking. "I'm sorry. . . . We'll fight, you know. The vision of the revolution was better than this. Ethiopia shouldn't be a dictatorship. We're too good for that."

Rolling Stone, September 21, 1978

THE WILDERNESS OF HOWLING ZEAL

A light climbs the back of a peak in Saudi Arabia to illuminate Sinai: an auroral orange warning precedes a sun that ascends like a brilliant shard of flaming metal, and in an instant, the world becomes searingly and unbearably hot. The light sweeps beyond the lapis Gulf of Aqaba and illuminates the mountainous southern massif of the ancient, empty peninsula, shaped like a spearhead sitting uneasily between Asia and Africa, between—especially today— Egypt and Israel. The granite peaks briefly flash their startling reds and blacks before they are so bleached of color by the light that the desert interior appears less like an earthly place than like an X ray of place.

Some soft, comprehensible middle ground that should rest between opposites is missing in Sinai. There is an unmitigated collision of night and day, color and colorlessness, desert and sea. Beliefs, convictions, even hunches there become howling zeal. Wars are all unimaginable bloodbaths. And when they emerge from the desert, the travelers, soldiers, and prophets who have come to Sinai for 5,000 years have always debated whether it is the place most forsaken by the god of the time or the place where God lives.

We drove south toward the sharp point of the great desert that morning, following a fossilized reef on the southeastern shore of the peninsula. We turned right, west, into the blazing rubble and refracted heat of the interior because we thought there would be a natural route through the granite walls that would lead to the blacktop road that the Israelis had built.

We found ourselves looking for a wadi that a Bedouin tribesman had told us would eventually take us to the road. Wadis are rough, circuitous saw cuts through desert mountains. They look just as you think a dried riverbed should look, though no river has flowed through Sinai within living memory. The canyons are parched except for one or two days of those rare years when, in keeping with the antipodal extremes in Sinai, the wadis course with murderous, bubbling flash floods that roll boulders, palm trees, and entire Bedouin encampments up to 30 miles toward the sea.

We plowed through the camel-colored dust of the alluvial fan at the seaward edge of a small wadi that we had decided was the right one. On the open plain, little silos of haze whirled slowly in the distance, mixing the green, orange, and brown sands that continually shift across the land.

As the wadi narrowed, its massive rock walls displayed the sharp, delicate, and splintered violence that is replicated in varying degrees throughout southern Sinai. The hills lie at broken angles to everything around them, sedimentary lines all turned sideways and pointing down toward the specific fault that twisted them. Shining black doleritic stripes called dykes, some an inch wide and others spanning 50 feet, streak the granite where shafts of molten magma shouldered their way into cracks and rose toward the sky. The whole landscape is still ringing in the afterglow of a geological trauma some six million years old that folded it until it snapped; the southern Sinai is old, but not the least bit elegant in its old age. The middle part of Sinai, the El Tih Plateau, is a desert where there is nothing save an array of canyons. ("There must be something," I said to a soldier who had spent a lot of time roaming it. "No," he said rather coldly, "there is nothing.") North of the El Tih there are dunes, the strategic passes of Sinai, and the meager population centers along the Mediterranean coast.

We couldn't tell if we'd gone a long way into the wadi or even if we'd been gone a long time; 9 A.M. in the open desert becomes midafternoon if you do anything other than sit. The heat makes you numb to appetite and other metabolic imperatives. You drink water because you are supposed to, though even thirst is easy to lose in the heat. For all my different activities in Sinai, I can't remember sweating once. A dryness seems to tighten your lips across your teeth so you can't even talk. You wear a hat because the sun can melt the water out of your head in minutes. Aaron Weingrod, my traveling companion, spoke of a day in Sinai when the temperature vaulted past 130 degrees and one member of his group had to pour water on the others to keep them all conscious. Aaron learned about the desert as a member of the Israeli paratroops.

In the midst of such reverberating heat, a certain resonance of thought occurs. It seems reasonable that men who left real lives in other places should wander into grandiose myth in Sinai. T. E. Lawrence and even Moshe Dayan were late on a list of military giants—both figurative and, very early, literal giants—who stepped blithely from real history at the edge of the desert straight into the fabulous. In the heat, I saw how somebody could flee the highly documented Bronze Age world of Ramses II and come here to chat with God about fundamental rules.

Further into the slender defile there were plants. Since it was summer, the most delicate and ephemeral of times in the desert, large, spindly plants fell over and uprooted as we brushed past them, falling over so easily and sadly that it was amazing that a breeze hadn't done it beforehand. Lush caper plants leaned out of the highest cracks in the rocks, stuffed into the crevices like rolled prayers in the Wailing Wall in Jerusalem.

The vegetation increased as we began to climb up a steep gulch. Near some stunted palm trees a little boy sat and sang shrill Bedouin grace notes to the other side of the canyon. Small goats and the young Bedouin's sisters came running toward us. The girls wrapped their black *khirges* around their heads and asked us for tobacco and rolling papers. They pulled the cloth over their noses and mouths in Muslim modesty, but their dark eyes all squinted smiles.

We followed an antique irrigation system up a steep incline to look for water. Air, moisture, plant life, all seemed to gather in this one spot. We found a filmy brown pool and collapsed alongside it to dump hatfuls of water on our heads. As we lay back, several ripe dates fell from the palm trees and landed ludicrously near our hands.

Then we heard splashing. We got up and walked toward the strange sound until Aaron stopped and began to laugh. Some ingenious father had, with bricks and stones, constructed a cistern in which a girl of 12 or so was standing naked and squealing and splashing, droplets of water sailing into the dry air all around her. When she saw us, the girl froze and quickly knitted her brown fingers into a veil for her dripping, grinning, naked face.

—

In 1956, General Moshe Dayan found some primitive arrowheads unearthed by the tread of a Sherman tank on its way to the other side of the desert as part of the Sinai campaign. It is hard to tell from his memoir of the event what Israel's most famous amateur archaeologist and current foreign minister made of the ancient weapons— which he thought to be between 6,000 and 8,000 years old—or if he took the discovery to be irony or affirmation at all.

War has rarely left Sinai. As if by historical agreement, the desert juncture has served as a battleground where countless generations wandered, looking for a fight. Wars there always uncover the refuse of older wars, and arrowheads join countless land mines, bullets, and skeletons that are everywhere under the sand. Sinai's famous holy history pales beside the unholy histories of civilizations exhibiting their least civilized aspects by sending their young men there to die.

The great invaders all had to take Sinai to get from one place to another—Ramses II, Alexander, Omar, Saladin, and even Napoleon all fought there. The Crusaders held parts of Sinai as feudal districts during the 12th century, long enough to rekindle the fanaticism of Islam, whose fanatics then stormed the other way. There were Romans, Persians, Byzantines, Saracens, Turks, and Arabs. The Jews of the Exodus first tasted organized combat at Refidim.

For 30 recent years of this century, two contiguous desert nations maintained the long tradition of fighting over this spearhead of empty land. Egyptian and Israeli soldiers battled for it five times. Sometimes the same men returned to fight over the same spot.

During the October war of 1973, when Egyptian forces crossed the Suez Canal into the Israeli-held Sinai, high-technology weapons were unsheathed that had never before been trundled into such an open, barren shooting gallery. They were the kinds of weapons that don't miss: wire-guided, laser-guided, and television-camera-guided. Computerized systems even made the dogfights in the clear air above Sinai a matter of straight shots of light between two pilots who couldn't see each other. More than 5,000 tanks went into battle, and some 3,000 were lost. Tension emanated so powerfully from Sinai that October that one morning people in the United States woke up to find the country in a state of nuclear alert. By the end of that war, Egypt's losses had brought its casualties since 1948 to an estimated total of 150,000 men. Enough became enough, and efforts were made to retire the battleground.

The five years of diplomatic effort that followed culminated in the Camp David agreement, which specified that control over Sinai should return to Egypt. Anwar el-Sadat had vowed to regain the peninsula, though even he must have doubted he could do it peacefully when he first said it. Now, having regained Sinai, Sadat wants to redeem it—by turning the 23,500 square miles of proving ground into a showcase of Third World development projects that will draw natural resources from the wilderness and make it home to millions of people. The Egyptians, in short, contend that they will carve a notch in the wilderness of Sinai.

For centuries, travelers who entered the place felt a need to say that they'd been there. The pharaohs erected stelae announcing that they'd done it again, and throughout the South certain walls are covered with ancient graffiti—some of them representing the earliest record of alphabetic symbols—where slaves and wanderers also surrendered to the compulsion to record their presence in such a place.

But for all the death there, all of the occupations—some of them lasting several centuries—no society has ever left a substantial scratch on the indurate surface of Sinai, and when you look out over it, it seems incredible that any nation should even want to try.

"It is important that we finally put a cultural mark all over Sinai," one of the Egyptians who negotiated the peace treaty said to me in Cairo.

"If you give the Sinai identity, won't you be the first to do it in 5,000 years?"

"Yes," he said. "And we will."

After the Israelis captured Sharm el Sheikh, near the tip of Sinai, they officially renamed it Ophira. But everyone there still calls it Sharm. Amos Goren sat outside a small house on a rise over one of the two bays at Sharm. He is a young man with the general proportions of an armored personnel carrier. He wore khaki shorts and a cutoff yellow sweatshirt bearing the image of an ibex, one of the last animals living in any numbers in all of Sinai. Amos was the kind of kid who ran on the organized 15-mile hikes. He used to bury M-80 fireworks in a sandy mound at the beach and scream, "This is the Aswan Dam!" before the mound blew up. He became an accomplished soldier in a country of accomplished soldiers. Then he left the army and came straight to Sinai to work for the Nature Reserves Authority, the powerful Israeli police force that protects the natural beauty of the peninsula with a near legendary zeal.

"You know, I've found some new things in there, and that's hard to do," Amos said, nodding toward the mountains. "I've seen places that no white man has ever seen in there." Amos says that after living in the open frontier space of Sinai, he can't spend two days in Tel Aviv without needing to flee. Since he can't live in the small space of Israel, he plans to go to South America "or somewhere" when Sharm is finally returned to Egypt in 1982 and he has to leave Sinai.

As the light faded and the famous Sinai night full of stars appeared, Amos folded an automatic weapon, jumped into his bright green jeep, and went out to stop his Bedouin friends from poaching sleeping lobsters off the reef.

—

Despite the forbidding summer heat, the mountains of southern Sinai were filled with young Israelis making what they feared would be one last trip to the wilderness. Groups of soldiers waited for hours in the pulsing sun to get jeep rides into the interior. The allure of Sinai for Israelis is that it is one of the few available escapes from what one writer has called the "latent hysteria" of the tiny, pent-up ball of Middle Eastern energy that is Israel. "Israel is a place with a six-day work week, rampaging inflation, and the possibility of wars on all sides," Aaron Weingrod had said as we drove toward Sinai. "It's a country that kills off almost as many people on the roads every year [620 in 1978] as it lost in the 1967 war." When the Israelis acquired Sinai in that war, the total area of their country quadrupled in a few days, and the nation experienced a revelation, a flip of the pressure valve.

Now Sinai is being returned to Egypt in slices, Kissingerian increments. While I was there, one more area was returned—a desert region next to the oil-producing district on the western shore that reverted to Egypt earlier. Some people in Israel bemoaned the lost revenues from the oil. Others, notably ranking military men, spoke of the cost of compressing the immense defense system they had built over all of Sinai into the comparatively tiny Negev Desert. The army would soon have less room in which to flex its muscles.

But to those who have spent time in Sinai, the loss is different. "There's a power here," one hiker explained at the foot of a mountain peak. The young man wore a beltful of canteens and toted a Kalashnikov assault rifle that his father had picked up in another part of Sinai in another era. "The loss of this place," he said, sweeping his hand toward the mountains and the space between them, "will be to me as a human being, not as an Israeli."

—

Amos took us on his rounds one day near the coastal oasis of Nabek, just up the shore from Ras Muhammad, where the tongue of the Red Sea splits like a snake's. We stopped for tea at the hut of one of the Bedouin families and were entertained by a gracious old man who often worked for Amos as a tracker. The hut was made of palm branches, cardboard, pieces of corrugated steel, newspapers, and an old bank of gymnasium lockers that had been painted yellow.

"He's very special," Amos said as we drove away. "He knows Sinai better than anyone here. He was a smuggler and knows the desert from Saudi Arabia to Ethiopia. I've taken him through places he hasn't visited in 20 years and he has it all in his head perfectly. He doesn't even know what a map is."

Having felt the disorientation that can entrap you in the labyrinth of the interior, I asked Amos if he knew how the Bedouin found their way "through the middle of nowhere."

"It's only nowhere to you," he said.

A Bedouin man appeared, walking determinedly across the coral sand ahead of us. He deliberately stopped in the path of Amos's jeep and flagged us down. The man was halfway in the jeep before I realized that he was blind. He wore traditional Bedouin garb, enhanced by modern accoutrements common to most Sinai Bedouin who work close to a modern outpost: a large-faced wristwatch, a Papermate pen, and a huge radio-cassette player. (The last item in particular is one that many Bedouin carry—often covered with bright, spangled radio covers made by their wives—as if in parody of the Israeli addiction to small transistor radios with which to listen to the hourly news.) We drove along for several miles with the man hunched in the back of the jeep until he said, "Stop." Then he got out, smiled, and strolled away, like a man who could see exactly where he was going.

Israeli researchers claim that the standard of living among the Bedouin tribesmen of southern Sinai—of whom there are no more than 6,000—has been raised by 350 percent over the 12 years of Israeli governance. Medical authorities report that their average lifespan has increased dramatically: it used to be barely over 30. The Bedouin are switching from camel herds to four-wheel-drive trucks. The herds have decreased partly because rising grain costs are making them expensive and partly because the young men who traditionally herded the camels can now find better work in construction or service industries along the coast. Amos says the younger generation is losing its desert skills and that it's increasingly difficult to find a tracker who's still in good enough shape to go out for ten days. A Bedouin acquaintance of Aaron's named Jamal recently changed his name to Jimmy, bought a guitar, left his wife and children in the desert, and followed a Swedish woman to Stockholm.

Amos expressed his disdain for the "Bedouin cult," the romanticism with which many Israelis seem to regard the desert Arabs. The earliest Jewish settlers in Palestine were just as enchanted by the Bedouin as were upper-class Englishmen of the 19th century (who, had they been aware of this Jewish proclivity so like their own, might have gone looking for a new culture to embrace). A man named Michael Halperin, a Zionist settler who arrived just after the turn of the century, traveled around encouraging Jews to marry Bedouin and convert them to Judaism. Early Jewish soldiers in Palestine even dressed like Bedouin, and to this day some young Israelis in Sinai often dress in desert garb and live near Bedouin encampments, wanting nothing more than to be the Bedouin's friend. "They romanticize their honesty, for instance," Amos said. "But the Bedouin steal, they lie—they're just people."

Some Israelis seemed to think that Bedouin life itself is threatened by the impending return of Egyptian rule, but almost every Bedouin shrugs at it. After all, they have lived under many different rulers—Israeli, Egyptian, British, and Turkish just in this century. But while I was in Sinai, Bedouin fishermen were seen salting and storing quantities of fish on the beach, guaranteeing a food supply for the future in a way they hadn't felt necessary for ten years.

—

Among the very few people who wandered into Sinai without preparing to do battle were the Greek monks who came in order to be alone in the wilderness early in the fourth century. During the subsequent invasions of the peninsula, these monks were repeatedly slaughtered, the most terrible massacres occurring at the hands of the Saracens in the fourth and fifth centuries. Finally, in 527, the Byzantine emperor Justinian built the monks a monastery-fortress, later called St. Catherine's, in which to take refuge—and varying numbers of Greek Orthodox ascetics have continued to reside there to this day.

In the months after it was announced that St. Catherine's would be returned to Egypt in November—an event that Sadat had promised to mark with a solemn flag-raising ceremony and the laying of a cornerstone for a combination mosque, Jewish temple, and Christian church—the ancient monastery was inundated with Israeli tourists. On the day that I visited St. Catherine's, Israelis stood shoulder to shoulder in the shimmering heat on the road to the monastery, most of them sporting the red Chico Marx hat called *kova tembel,* the Israeli national headgear.

But things have changed at St. Catherine's since the days when pilgrims emerged from the desert and collapsed in tears into the waiting monks' arms chanting "Salve Regina," and when a bottle of brandy would secure a visitor an invitation to stay for a week. A year ago, angry Israeli tourists broke down the gate of the monastery when the fewer than 12 monks who still live inside became overwhelmed with their numbers and locked them out. And during my visit several monks, looking pale under their long beards, paced about unhappily near the gorgeous sixth-century wooden doors of the Church of the Transfiguration, clearly nervous over the size of the tourist throng. The monks had closed off several of the more famous rooms of the monastery, which angered the crowd in one small courtyard—a crowd that included a small boy toting an AK-47 rifle ("Don't point it, I told you," his mother yelled) and an Israeli soldier wearing a lovely flowered dress he'd borrowed in order to cover his legs and pass the monks' dress code. The Israelis' eagerness, however, was balanced by skepticism. They couldn't quite believe that Moses really received the Ten Commandments on a nearby mountain (one of six claimants to the title of Mount Sinai), let alone that the foliage outside one chapel is the living descendant of the bush that burned with God's presence.

The monastery library was once the resting place of the famed Codex Sinaiticus, a fourth-century translation of the Bible into Greek that is now in the British Museum. The library still contains most of the major documents and illuminations sacred to Byzantine Christendom, all housed on a hilltop that will soon pass from the rule of the Jews to that of the Muslims. This, however, is an eventuality for which St. Catherine's is at least partially prepared, for the monks also have a letter signed by Muhammad's nephew and bearing the prophet's fingerprint. This document, apparently forged to impress earlier generations of Islamic invaders, thanks some of the monks' predecessors for the hospitality they showed Muhammad during a visit.

—

On the way from Israel into northern Sinai, we passed through the Gaza Strip, where young Palestinians congregated on street corners in the towns. The peace symbolized by the return of Sinai to Egypt, and indeed the peace within Sinai, can be locked in only by the successful resolution of the myriad issues of Gaza and the West Bank. The people of those areas say they want a Palestinian homeland, perhaps a Palestinian state. But they are now earning more money than they've ever had by working in Israel, building Israel, being the proletariat of Israel. Aaron called such dependence on Arab labor "the downfall of Zionism" and said: "It wasn't supposed to be like that."

We were going to visit a Sinai settlement on the Mediterranean—a place called Sufa, where Aaron had been stationed after
his stint in the paratroops. First it was a *nachal*-kibbutz, an encampment of uniformed soldier-farmers who tended a small vegetable garden and conducted armed patrols of the beaches and the
Arab villages. Then the tents gave way to cement buildings, the
uniforms disappeared, the name was changed from Sukot to Sufa,
and the place became a home for new pioneers of the conquered
desert—part of a system intended to plant thousands of Israelis
along the northern axis of Sinai. Now, with the new peace, the Sinai
settlers will have to move.

Before we reached Sufa, some Israeli soldiers flagged us down at
a junction outside the large settlement town of Yamit, a few miles
from the town of El Arish, which had just been returned to Egypt.
Behind the soldiers, trucks and piles of tires were burning, and several cement mixers were parked across the highway in an im-
promptu barricade. Children ran in and out of the large crowd that
had assembled in the area, and people swirled around one another in
evident confusion. On the other side of the blockade, Israeli military
trucks bearing bits of dismantled army outposts waited in a line
with a variety of white United Nations vehicles. There was a lot of
running and screaming and violent waving of arms and sticks. The
residents of Yamit had that morning decided that the Israeli government had taken too long in offering them fair compensation for the
homes they would have to vacate.

A man named Dov seemed to be running things. He said that he
owned the supermarket in Yamit and had lived there since 1974,
when his wife returned from a meeting in Philadelphia all aglow
with the idea of being a frontier settler. Dov wore a powder-blue
T-shirt and a sailor's hat with blue palm trees on it that said, "Welcome to Yamit." He was visibly upset and talked fast: "Begin comes
out here and says, 'We are making some sacrifices for peace and you
people are my sacrifices. Only history will judge me,' he says. This
government is sick. Begin's dying. Dayan's dying. The snowball of
peace is melting in the sun. You'll see. People will stay here until the

end because we know that they'll see that we are dealing with liars in the Egyptians. . . . This land passed to the Jews by blood!"

Later, rumors filtered in that an Israeli patrol had fired over the top of a Yamit resident's car. Dov came running over and pulled my tape recorder up to his mouth. "We have weapons, too," he hissed. "If you shoot, it's gonna go bloody!"

Aaron and I left our car outside the burning roadblocks and hitchhiked into Yamit, once intended to be a little Tel Aviv in Sinai with 250,000 residents. The main square was deserted, and harsh De Chirico shadows sliced the empty sidewalks that run through the town. Yamit is a geometric conglomeration of what look like cement mobile homes that have been dropped in the sand. A weave of black hoses from the drip irrigation systems that snake throughout the cultivated area of northern Sinai lay in the tiny, obstinate gardens in front of each residence. Along the Sinai coast I saw places where an irrigation hose had been inadvertently kicked away from a plant, and the plant had desperately crawled through the sand to get back to the hose.

People in Yamit now speak of the conspiracies of the "Arab press and their Western allies," about "Arab capital" and its influence in the West, seemingly unaware of the perverse historical inversion of their claims. To justify their treatment of local Bedouin, who are not allowed in Yamit at certain hours and must constantly produce special identification, many of the Israeli residents of the town cite American treatment of the Indians. The town is divided into three groups, which express varying degrees of militancy about their plight. The most zealous of these groups has closed meetings, and its posters and bumper stickers are paid for by a mysterious group inside Israel proper. Dov, the man at the crossroads with his *Exodus* name and his threats of violent resistance to any attempt at dispossession, is not considered extreme.

At a far edge of Yamit is a war memorial known as the Monument. It commemorates the tank battles that took place in the area in 1967 and 1973. A fence encloses many cement pillars of varying diameters and heights. Atop each of the columns rests a piece of twisted military hardware. There are gun barrels, springs, crank-shafts, and riddled armor. In the middle of this technological grave-yard, rising higher than anything on the coast of northern Sinai, is a modern tower with a spiral staircase. From the top of the monument we could see Bedouin tents that skirted the beach up to Sufa. In the other direction there was smoke from a burning car at the cross-roads. Below, the wind whistled through the holes in the relics on top of the pedestals. The place held a confusing power. The Egyptians have said that they have no intention of living with such a symbol, that they will tear it down.

I had requested to be "passed across" to the Egyptians at El Arish, which is just a few minutes from Yamit. But despite the pronouncements of Begin and Sadat that there is to be free passage across the borders, it turned out this will not become a reality until January. "The first wave [of Israelis] will probably be the conquerors anyway," an Egyptian diplomat said later. "It'll be the carpetbaggers, the big shots looking to make money, businessmen and the loudmouths. I'm not looking forward to it, so what's the hurry?"

So I would have to fly to Athens and come back through Cairo to get just a few miles across Sinai. Some Yamit residents took me aside when they heard I was headed to El Arish to tell me of the brutal execution on the El Arish beach of one William, the owner of a popular local tavern known as the Hilton. (At the time, Israeli newspapers were carrying many stories about an alleged Egyptian crackdown on Arab residents of El Arish who had worked with Israelis.) I asked why William had been shot.

"Because he served Jews *food!*" a woman said, her voice cracking.

The Yamitans, heirs to a dream that somehow came down to subsidized beach villas, saw conspiracies everywhere around them. Everywhere in Sinai, in fact, there were symbols and messages and people looking for them. In another, more beautiful part of the peninsula, a young man quietly took me aside and talked of something I'd already observed. "As a reporter, you should find out why all the Israeli flags here are ripped in the same place. Something's going on," he said. "You should find out what the rips mean." Eventually, I found that the flags had all been ripped by the Sinai winds. "Flags make the wind," the Israeli poet Yehuda Amichai once wrote. "The wind doesn't make the wind."

———

The Israelis call the pre-1967 border between Israel and Sinai the green line. In Cairo, I learned there really *is* a green line. In his impressive Cairo headquarters, Dr. M. A. Abdel Hady leaned over a set of colorful transparencies and traced it with his finger. There was no bitterness; it is a scientific matter. A picture from a Landsat satellite, beefed up with the aid of Hady's sophisticated remote sensing procedures, shows that a heavy green line really does run along the political border between Israel and Sinai. Seen from space, Israel is green and Sinai has no color. "It's not cultivation either," Hady said. "It's a very interesting phenomenon that's worth investigating. It is partly because of the conservation of the surface soil, protection from overgrazing and less erosion."

The Remote Sensing Center is the jewel of Egyptian developmental technology. Hady's system enhances topographical images by computer and is probably the only area in which Egyptian technology is substantially ahead of Israel's.

Under the glass of Hady's coffee table were innumerable photographs of Anwar el-Sadat sitting next to Hady in that very room. With fine bureaucratic talent, Hady parlayed his special skills, a grant from the U.S. National Science Foundation, and an uncanny resemblance to Henry Kissinger into a scientific establishment that boasts an airborne lab, computers, and the support of more than one president. Since 1974, he has produced maps of Sinai that depict every wrinkle, crack, and soil gradation in the peninsula, and his work could provide a comprehensive underpinning for Egyptian schemes to turn the Sinai Desert into a garden.

One of these schemes is to draw substantial quantities of coal, oil, manganese, gypsum, and various other minerals from Sinai. Another involves the cultivation of two million acres in central Sinai using underground aquifers, and the opening up of 250,000 more acres in the dunes of northern Sinai using wells and runoff retention systems. The crowning achievement—if all goes as hoped—will be the relocation of some two million Egyptians in Sinai within 20 years.

All this rests on a vision of Egypt that could come only from Anwar el-Sadat, a testimony to the breadth of his imagination. He sees peace not as an end in itself but as a step toward the reconstruction of a country that has never achieved its acknowledged potential. Once the economy is demilitarized—which Egyptian officials say will not happen before the return of Sinai is completed in 1982—and conditions for investment improve, greenery, according to Sadat, "will cover the entire Sinai peninsula." This unprecedented development is planned for a country whose population, now 41 million, is increasing by 1 million every 10 months; a country where 99 percent of the people live on 4 percent of the land, and the cultivable soil is decreasing all the time. There is a special audacity— perhaps even a foolhardiness—in the idea of a nation tackling Sinai after being dragged into some of the worst years of its long history by commitments to projects it couldn't afford.

I had just come out of the Sinai peninsula and had stood in that sun and examined the rock and the dust that is so far from soil that Sadat's idea would never even come to mind. The whole thing seemed fantastic. In contrast to Israeli authorities, who didn't seem to want to talk about any aspect of Sinai, the Egyptians all wanted to tell of their plans. There was a sense of bounding, renascent élan.

The headquarters of the Desert Research Institute is housed in the former mansion of one of King Farouk's more decadent cousins in northern Cairo. There one of the authors of the documents upon which Sadat based the plans for his so-called Green Revolution, an agronomist named Dr. Muhammad Atef Abdel Salam, laid out goals somewhat more modest than those expressed by Sadat. Dr. Salam noted that many reservations expressed by the institute were not included in the government's publicity for the Green Revolution. He admitted, too, that the intensive efforts to reach—or even to understand—the reservoir of water known to exist deep under the New Valley area in Egypt's Western Desert, a region far more accessible than Sinai, have so far proved fruitless; yet work on that project began back in 1959 and has received assistance from the Soviet Union and the United States.

Contrary to many predictions, moreover, transfers of data between leading Israeli and Egyptian scientists have been limited. As a result, there is an entire generation of young Israeli Sinai specialists who fear they will soon have no place to study. A three-volume compilation of some of their work, including studies on everything from climate and the creation of pastures to patterns of shark behavior, is currently being prepared, and I arrived in Cairo with requests from several Israeli scientists to try to make contact for them with an Egyptian counterpart so that they could continue their work. But I soon sensed that the Egyptians resented the requests. "The Israelis were never farmers before the 1940s," one Egyptian said, "while we Egyptians have been farmers for a thousand years. They can't compete with us in farming—only in new techniques."

"It's like they did after they got Palestine," scoffed an Egyptian official, a high-ranking engineer. "They said that they got the desert and made a paradise, but that's a big lie. A big lie! Because Palestine was already cultivated and full of food. They are just good at bragging." And at least ten Egyptians told me that the roads the Israelis built in Sinai will last only two more years. They say this proves that the Israelis knew they would have to return the desert peninsula, but it was hard to tell whether they were glad the new roads were inferior, or unhappy that they would have to build them all over again.

To some extent, all this simply reflects an ultrasensitivity born of living with the international image of Israeli expertise in desert technology. But it is true that the Egyptians did begin to develop Sinai themselves during the 1950s. They built roads and drilled oil fields—and in 1967, just as their new ferromanganese mine was due to go into operation, the Israelis took the peninsula and dismantled the equipment.

In a lobby of the Ministry of Development and New Communities building in Cairo is a huge model of a desert city to be constructed by the year 2000 in Egypt's Western Desert. Despite the Egyptians' desire to get out from under the shadow of Israeli prestige in desert development, this model looks exactly like Yamit multiplied by some exponential power. Hundreds of white cubes are broken only by the spires of three mosques. The shape and the size—the settlement is intended to be home to one million Egyptians—are probably omens of the future of Sinai as well.

"Why Sinai?" I asked the chairman of the government's joint development committee. "Aren't there parts of Egypt that are closer, have better soil, and would be less hard on settlers—"

"That's true," he cut in. "But when I pick something from your pocket and then you get it back from me, somehow you find that you need to put a sign on it."

"Sinai was never in the hearts of the Egyptian people," Muhammad Ahmed Makram, one of Cairo's leading journalists, said, "but I was moved by the Jews trying to live with Sinai, to know the Bedouin like that, and to build there. Our young people were moved by it, too. Now Sinai can be a place for our young."

But there is simply no tradition of living in the wilds in Egypt. Even without Sinai, the country is 90 percent desert, and for several millennia no Egyptians have seen any sense to leaving the Nile Valley. And the problem of finding settlers for Sinai will surely be complicated by the fact that over a million Egyptians now work abroad, particularly in the Gulf states. A young Egyptian with the itch to play settler can do so in Kuwait and become relatively rich in the process. Sadat may offer substantial plots of sandy land to the people, but never riches.

—

The young translator from the Egyptian State Information Service came in for a lot of kidding when his colleagues learned that he was to accompany me to Sinai. Ahmed usually worked at the press center in Cairo with several other translators, all of whom seemed to have studied with the same inspirational professor of English literature. In between my appointments with Egyptian authorities, and every time we stopped during our trek through Egyptian Sinai, Ahmed launched into rapid-fire queries concerning my opinion of "Shockspeare," "Meal-tone," and "Ten-C-Williams."

Ahmed arrived on the morning of our departure for Sinai wearing a natty sport shirt, a polyester sport coat, tinted glasses, and very shiny shoes. I was amazed to find that in sharp contrast to the Israeli trekkers, with their khaki shorts, sun hats, and hiking boots, many Egyptians entering the desert wore high-style Sadat suits.

The floating bridge at Qantara is supposed to swing from its resting place on the west bank of the Suez Canal and stretch across to the other side at ten in the morning—which was when Ahmed and I arrived there. By two in the afternoon, the bridge still had not opened, and there was a very long line on both sides of the "long ditch," as the British used to call it—a line that included army trucks, gas trucks, and a fleet of run-down pickups bearing vegetables that were cooking in the sun. The tomatoes were blistered, and the smell of stewed fruit mixed with the hot dust in the air. Watermelons imploded from the heat. Babies screamed from under trucks, and people stood on the roofs of their cars. There were many ancient, elongated Mercedes in the line; in Israel they are called Arab taxis. The cars were jammed with people, blankets, tires, chickens, pigeons, and usually had chairs and sofas secured to the roof. The headlights and grillwork of both the taxis and the vegetable trucks were covered with a peculiarly Islamic latticework that looked like patterns from a mosque window.

Most of the people in the taxis were moving back to El Arish after 12 years of what all of them called exile. In a matter of days after El Arish's turnover by the Israelis, the population of Sinai's only real town had jumped from 35,000 to more than 100,000—twice the population before 1967. Though most Egyptians found the normal birthrate sufficient explanation for this population surge over little more than a decade, it appears that a portion of the new population can be traced to the large number of civil servants dispatched to El Arish by the Egyptian government and the numerous skilled laborers who rushed there looking for work.

A young vegetable vendor named Abu Muhammad was eight when the Israelis rolled in to El Arish. Now a handsome young man of 20, he bragged about the various countries to which his vegetables traveled as Israeli exports. Abu had lived most of his life under Israeli rule, and many of his friends were Israelis. I asked if he felt Egyptian.

"At first I didn't," he said. "But I learned. There's a place out there where I used to work called Yamit where they just hate Egyptians. They hated me, so I learned what I was." He looked at his vegetables, which were now cracking in the heat. "I sure wish Allah would let us cross."

Eventually, Allah did, and we headed toward El Arish. A motley single-track road winds out of Qantara and enters the dunes of northwestern Sinai. The "road" is little more than a slender meeting of tar patches and pools of sand that circumvent the giant sand dunes that are in the process of obliterating the original roadbed.

At a small oasis called Bir al Abd that the Green Revolution is supposed to turn into an agricultural town of 50,000, a Bedouin in a small store complained that he was money out of pocket since the Israelis left. He said that fishing is off and that the Bedouin were trying to reorganize their flocks. The man stood under a huge Egyptian flag and said to Ahmed that he welcomed the Egyptians and hoped that tourism would bring back his business.

"His business is smuggling," Ahmed said with disgust as we got back in the car.

The relative loyalty of the northern Sinai Bedouin is the subject of much conjecture in Egypt. Every Egyptian knows of the events of the 1956 Sinai war, when thousands of Egyptian soldiers, abandoned by their officers, tried to walk 50 miles across the sand to El Arish. They were found later with their throats cut and uniforms stripped off—supposedly by local Bedouin.

At the outskirts of El Arish, I was briefly detained by the first of many secret policemen I would meet, a startlingly tall Egyptian decked out in sunglasses, a paisley shirt, a green, luminous-faced digital watch, and a gigantic gun that protruded from his pants. He stared into my eyes for a while across a rickety table. Ahmed flitted around nervously, attesting to my credentials and smoking Cleopatra cigarettes. The man allowed us to pass but said we had to go directly to the intelligence police headquarters, where I was detained for another half hour.

El Arish is a hilly, palm-filled town made up of small, ramshackle houses. In the yard of every house and next to the roads and all along the beach there were tents. Amazingly, families returning to their homes after 12 years away simply moved in with the people who had lived there during the Israeli occupation. According to official estimates, it will cost $40 million to rehouse all of the former residents of El Arish.

The ancient caravan city is a kind of unreconstructed Australia of the desert, a 2,700-year-old penal colony that transmogrified quite slowly into a smuggling center. It is also, improbably, the place where Menachem Begin and Anwar el-Sadat met to open the "way of peace" together. Posters of Sadat depicted from every conceivable angle stretch across many of the streets. "With sweat and toil we will reconstruct beloved Egypt," some of them say.

Most great armies crossing Sinai have built forts or at least stopped to rest in El Arish. Many of Napoleon's soldiers were stricken with plague here, and that experience, coupled with their defeat at Acre, helped decide the French to leave the desert to someone else. Back in 1902, Theodor Herzl suggested to the British that in view of the comparative fertility of the oasis, El Arish might serve as a suitable homeland for the Jews.

I claimed extreme hunger as we left the secret police compound in town and suggested we eat at a restaurant that had been recommended to me by some Israelis. The place proved to be the only restaurant in El Arish that was known as the Hilton and hence—I assumed—must have been owned by the lately executed feeder of Israelis, William. As it turned out, I found William there alive and feeding Egyptians. After identity checks, I told Subhi "William" Kalam, a small, very dark

Egyptian, that his loyal former patrons back in Israel believed him to be dead—at which he looked upset. Later I overheard some Egyptian officials discussing William's unusually high standard of living and the fact that he seemed to have endless supplies of Israeli macaroni. When I told William that, he smiled comfortably.

The Egyptians admittedly overlook an unprecedented renaissance in the art of smuggling that has occurred in Sinai since El Arish was returned. The line that will split Sinai until 1982 will run right down the center, from El Arish to Ras Muhammad. There were already stories of entire fleets of trucks being buried in the sand just before the Israeli northern territory became Egyptian again. Great smuggling cultures have always lived within formidable natural barriers between two economies. Though the Bedouin have been at the smuggling trade for less time than, for instance, the Basques, their reputation is nonetheless legendary. Hashish is customarily the main product moved across the sand, but lately, with radical differences in living standards suddenly foisted on many people, the demand for food has been skyrocketing on the Egyptian side.

In the back of William's restaurant, I met a man who showed me a bulging wallet full of Israeli money. He smilingly explained that he held a regular job in Tel Aviv to which he commuted through a minefield every day. "I make 40 Egyptian pounds a day in a hotel there," he said. "If the Egyptians think I'm going to give that up, they're crazy."

William relaxed after a while, and at a long table full of Egyptian government men, he began to tell the story of his life, dwelling heavily on the time that he talked the Israelis into giving him back his home, money, and restaurant after they'd confiscated it. The officials were all amused. William then talked about the new restaurant he planned to open to accommodate the tourist boom he predicted when the Israeli-Egyptian border finally opens. It will be a downmarket companion to the Hilton, "with plastic and everything," that William intends to name Wimpy.

All the officials in El Arish—including the various intelligence men I met—insisted that I go to see a farm that was surrendered by the Israelis when El Arish was "liberated" by the peace accords. The farm was outside Neot, a settlement inhabited by religious zealots belonging to the right-wing Israeli group called Gush Emunim—the Bloc of the Faithful. Last May, when they were told they would have to stop farming the patch of land that reverted to Egypt, the Gush Emunim settlers fought Israeli soldiers with stones and cans of chemical insecticides.

The kibbutz at Neot remains in Israeli hands. The farm that went to Egypt was still a mess when I was there. Several groups of young Egyptians stood around nodding their heads in sorrowful agreement as an engineer showed me the scorched fields, the plugged water well, the severed irrigation hoses, the Hebrew graffiti, and the pump house that had been blown to bits by the departing Israelis. The man told me that the "Jews even plugged our oil wells in the South"— which wasn't true, although some of them have apparently been damaged by overpumping. "Look at what the Jews have done," the man said as he swept his arm over the charred blocks of cement buildings.

"Which Jews did this?" I asked.

"The Israelis," he said. "And Jews didn't even build these wells. We did—well, some Americans helped. It was a research project. But Jews didn't."

Neot bore no signs of reconstruction or salvage work. The only worker in action while I was there turned out to be an American Mennonite volunteer.

Before I left El Arish, a security policeman inflicted one final interview upon me; he was sitting under a newly designed flag for Sinai, which is triangular and fringed, with a yellow background over which are arranged an olive branch, oil derricks, a fish, and some gears. "Is that the olive branch of peace?" I asked the security man.

"I think it's the symbol of agriculture," he said thoughtfully.

As we drove over an Israeli road, wide as an airstrip ("They wanted it for planes in emergencies," Ahmed said), that has now become an Egyptian road and is soon to be the "way of peace," small foxes kept crossing in front of our headlights. We came upon a hut and some parked cars where there were men with rifles and women crying. An Egyptian policeman with a long stick was whacking a very tall Bedouin man whose long arms were wrapped around himself. The man, who had been caught smuggling, was spinning around as the policeman hit him, and as he spun, another man pulled at his robes. Yelling and dancing, the smuggler spun faster and faster, and through the flicker of the headlights we saw Teflon frying pans, toasters, electric fans, candy bars, jewelry, and whole sides of meat falling to the sand at his feet.

—

A learned Egyptian turned to me one day in Cairo. "One thing about the peace," he said, shaking his head. "Jews don't make very good neighbors. When I was studying at Columbia, my friend had a miserly Jewish landlady, and he told me all about what she was like. So I don't know about the Jews." Then he continued to outline his plans to make the desert bloom. This man had been commissioned to rehabilitate an ancient desert partly just to show some Jews that his people could do it. It seemed incredible that he had to base his image of people who live quite literally just down the road on a woman in far-off New York City who probably couldn't say "thank you" in Hebrew.

Pride appears on both sides of Sinai, and it has inspired an envy in the Egyptians nearly as big as their vision. In the end, that vision seems to differ little from some of the less admirable historical visions that have brought so many men to Sinai, so often just to die. It was as if the Egyptians were back on the Sinai battlefield, dragging their honor onto the barren desert to see if it could survive in the sun.

The return of the Egyptians to Sinai sends a charge through the web of nerves that carries the mystique of Israeli power. The mystique still compels many Israelis to declare that if the Egyptians "don't behave," the proud army of the Jews will retake the Suez Canal "in a day"—a prediction that looks unlikely in the light of the 1973 war. It may be more important that, with Sinai gone, "all the tension will come back home to Israel," as one departing Israeli set-tler said. "After 30 years in a state of alert, peace will be the real trial for our country," he added.

It's quite something, this peace between two countries that—except for their armies—understand so little about each other. Yet sometimes their desires converge. Menachem Begin used to say that he intended to retire to Neot, to live out his final days symbolically in an Israeli-held Sinai. Anwar el-Sadat has gone him one better and announced his intention to be buried in Sinai, on that towering mountain where some people think Moses received the Word from God. Their two countries, each with an injured economy, each tor-mented by its own traumas, remain locked, shalom to salaam, within the bizarre geopolitical matrix that strings events in Sinai to a New Jersey voter sitting in a gas line.

For all the harsh collisions of symbols, tensions, and armies in Sinai, for all of the technologies dragged toward one another in the desert—first the technologies of war, then those of peace—the naked wilderness has thus far remained unchanged, its shattered landscapes unmarked by the fleeting times of peace and unstained by the bloody years of war. Sinai has always taunted the people who moved over it, or owned it, or wanted it, as if to declare that this wilderness will be subdued only after every other wilderness and wildness in the world has been mastered, too.

GEO, December 1979

THE HANS BRINKER COMPLEX

Hours before dawn we were arranged into long lines, and now 16,000 of us waited with sharp steel blades clutched in our hands like sabers.

We stood together in a great, bright hall that smelled of cattle and long winters. Vendors offered to sell us flashlights, since we would be skating in the dark for several hours. Some of the skaters looked young and lean in their racing suits, built like the best marathon runners, but just as many of the Dutchmen waiting in the Frieslandhal in the city of Leeuwarden that morning looked like they were heading off to work in the background of an old Dutch landscape painting, people grown thick and tough through years of work on land their ancestors stole from the sea.

For each of the last 22 winters, the legendarily skilled skaters of Holland had waited for the Elfstedentocht, the ice race of all races. The last "Eleven Towns" tour, a 124-mile-long circuit of the province of Friesland over frozen canals and inland lakes, had occurred so long ago that many of the skaters now waiting to begin the race grew up never seeing their national sporting event. The race had been held only 12 times during this century; the northern winters no longer seemed capable of producing a tract of solidified ice sufficiently hard and uninterrupted that thousands of people could travel it from darkness to darkness for all of a day. But each winter an entire nation of skaters still wiped the animal fat from their long touring blades and trained for an event that never came.

The Elfstedentocht had become less a race than a mythic component of the Dutch national unconscious, and as I stood in the great hall, trying to stay loose, I felt like an explorer who happened upon a native rite so private and strange and entwined in the secrets of history that all he could do was stand quietly aside and try to understand.

But for my choice of ice skates, I might have been anthropologically concealed in the crowd along with the handful of Swedes and Finns who'd been allowed to trespass on the hallowed ice for the first time in the history of the race. People kept coming up to me and staring at my hockey skates.

"You're the American," said a man with a long beard that already looked frozen. "I saw your picture in the paper." He had thick grease smeared on his face and wore bedroom slippers on his feet; his goggles wrapped around a wool skating cap that had clearly been knit at home. Like every other participant in the hall, his pants bulged out seven or eight inches around the knees from a lump of padding. I didn't fully understand the padding, though it had been suggested that some of the bridges along the course were so low that a skater would have to fall to his knees and slide through.

The man continued to stare at my short-bladed skates. "You are very courageous," he said, shaking his head.

"I think you are very stupid," said an older man behind him.

"Yes, well, this is also possible," said the first man upon consideration.

Word passed through the long lines that a million Dutch citizens were waiting outside the hall and along the banks of the route to cheer us on, and as the moment approached for the first group of skaters to run to the ice, the Frieslandhal seemed to rumble with a terrible thunder. Ninety percent of the Dutch population was expected to watch the Elfstedentocht from start to finish on television, leaving, I assumed, only the blind or comatose to miss the event. Offices and factories were shuttered throughout the country, and Queen Beatrix had rushed back from abroad when she heard the ice had thickened.

———

Groups of 1,000 skaters were released from the hall in half-hour intervals, starting at 5:30 A.M. At 6:30, my group tore the bottom stubs off of our *controlekaarten* and handed them to a race official as we rushed past him into the dark. The part we kept had blank spots next to the name of each of the 11 villages, to be stamped as we passed through.

Outside the hall, a slender chute divided the massive crowd. We began a tentative run over lightly iced ground that glistened under arc lights strung overhead. The violent light made silhouettes of the looming walls of faces and occasionally lit our skate blades bright as long, thin flames. The crowd was so close on either side that they warmed the wintry morning and filled the chute with amazing noise made of screams and bugle calls and cheers that fell into a rhythmic "hey! hey! hey!" The sound pummeled us from side to side like gusts of wind across a slick road.

Three-quarters of a mile later, at the edge of the van Harinxma Canal, I could see tugboats and flat-bottomed barges frozen into the ice up to their hulls. A thousand skaters piled down the dirt banks of the canal and sat side by side to put on skates. No one said a word, and it had become so quiet that I could hear the complaint of cold leather being stretched by strong laces.

As they set off, most skaters simply tossed their bedroom slippers, running shoes, and heavy wooden shoes behind them. In light of the possibility of finding oneself a province away with no shoes to wear, the gesture seemed to tempt fate. I slipped my shoes into my pack.

I skated slowly down to the base of the canal and watched others disappear into the blackness to the south. The ice was even blacker than the lightless morning and felt strange underfoot. The skates of the others made an unusually deep, roaring sound against the ice as they disappeared into the dark, like hundreds of coal cars falling fast into a mine.

I tested my laces, skated back and forth in a mild panic, and jumped up and down on the marble-hard ice in what I'm sure a psychologist would call a test of reality. I waited beneath a grain elevator that rose above the base of the canal until I saw the next group of a thousand skaters running through the sonic gauntlet of spectators toward the ice. As the first of them appeared on the rise at the edge of the canal, I took a breath and began to take long strides into the dense mist of an old dream.

———

As constant and unresolved as my Hans Brinker complex obviously was, my childhood fantasies of skating the canals of Holland had never included images of myself pitted in competition against 16,122 of the most powerful ice skaters in the world. For Hans it was the silver skates at the end of the race, but all I wanted were the glorious windmills I would pass along the banks of the canals.

I'd known about the famed tour through the 11 ancient villages of the northern province of Friesland in the Netherlands for a long time, and for years I'd badgered various Dutch government officials and journalists about calling me if the race were ever scheduled to take place. But along with 14 million *Nederlanders,* I'd finally given up the wait. Winter teased me and the people of the lowlands unmercifully for years. In 1975, the ice was so hard that skaters began to congregate in Friesland only to be informed that the ice was melting. The winter of 1984 was particularly cold, and in December the Elfstedentocht was scheduled, only to be canceled a few hours later. The ice was ready again in mid-January, but the temperature rose at the last minute. The latest the race had ever been held was on a February 14, back in 1956, and that was considered a meteorological freak. So by mid-February of 1985, all hope was lost, and the depression that attends spring along the canals had settled in.

Then on February 18, the nation was electrified by the announcement that the race was to be held in three days, on the 21st. Four busloads of Dutch skaters on their way to an alternative race in Poland turned around, and thousands of skaters stood in lines to register. For the first time, the race committee announced, a limited number of foreigners would be allowed to enter this 13th Elfstedentocht.

—

There was a great commotion at the KLM Airlines ticket counter when somebody noticed my skates. "It won't happen," one woman said. "It never does." But four hours after I got the phone call about the race, I was on a plane to Amsterdam, and eight hours after that, I boarded a packed train headed north to Leeuwarden.

Most of the people holding skates on the train looked as tired as I did because they'd spent up to 12 hours in the cold waiting to register. As the younger skaters sat together and talked strategy, the older men—I didn't see women with skates on the train but just under 300 did enter—sat together and talked of past races. Many of them already had an Elfstedentocht Cross, a decoration as valued by a Dutchman as any badge of courage earned in war. They talked about old Karst Leemburg, who won the 1929 race, but lost his toes to the cold—he still keeps them in a jar by his bed—and they remembered the last race, held in 1963 during a blizzard so cold that only 200 of the thousands of entrants finished. There is a famous photograph of that year's winner crossing the finish line, looking for all the world like a man frozen solid; Dutch schoolchildren wear that image emblazoned in their memories.

Everyone on the train pored over newspapers given over entirely to news of the race. There was much conjecture about whether the 30-year-old record of 7 hours, 35 minutes, would be broken, and most people agreed it would probably fall. Since the last Elfstedentocht, an entire semiprofessional sport called marathon skating had developed, replete with hundreds of world-class, full-time participants who regularly competed in races of more than 60 miles. These athletes were capable of skating at almost 20 miles an hour for much of a day. The favorite on the train was clearly the legendary Jan Roelof Kruithof. Known throughout northern Europe as "J.R.," Kruithof had won eight of the last nine annual alternative races held in northern Finland. He had spent every summer since the last Elfstedentocht working out in a meat locker, and he was quoted in the paper as believing that his entire career had been little more than training for the Eleven Towns race.

Another character named Hans Homme echoed Kruithof's praise of training in a freezer. The plainly mad-looking Mr. Homme made someone in his family lock him into a deep freeze, where he pedaled a stationary bicycle in front of a fan blowing a minus-6-degree wind in his face. "If you stop, you freeze and die," Homme contended in one article, "so it makes you pretty tough in the body and mind."

There were numerous bits about "Crazy Dries" van Wijhe, who abandoned all sophisticated strategies in favor of skating as fast as he could go until he dropped. Crazy Dries often won marathon races; he refused to skate on Sundays, however, because of his devout Calvinist convictions.

The newspapers universally described the course of the Elfstedentocht as "tortuous," and several groups on the train had large maps of the province of Friesland spread out on the floor. Though the official roots of the race extend back to 1909, the tour is descended from a 200-year-old practice among off-season *friese* farmers of skating to all of the 11 towns in one day in order to stop in each town and have a drink.

Friesland is home to descendants of one of the fiercest tribes in the ancient world. The Friezen were one of the three original groups of marsh dwellers who settled the lowlands that became the Netherlands, and the modern Friezen still speak an ancient language called Fries, which sounds more like Middle English than Dutch. The locals are further distinguished by their propensity toward skating like the wind, and by a rather straightforward, stiff demeanor that causes them to be the butt of a great deal of national humor. In the main square of the capital city of Leeuwarden, atop the pedestal usually occupied by a founding father or a war hero, sits a huge bronze statue of a cow that during the 19th century produced 6,620 pounds of milk in one year. People from more sophisticated regions of the Netherlands think this "perfect cow" of Leeuwarden is pretty funny stuff, but as the train finally arrived in Leeuwarden, and we hiked across the town to the staging center at the Frieslandhal, it was clear that everyone was Friezen—except me.

"Do you know you are the only American ever to enter the race?" one of the circle of reporters asked.

"No," I said. "I guess I was the only one who could get here."

"You're not representing America?"

"No, I just had a childhood fantasy . . ."

"Are you in training?"

"Well, not really."

"Do you know you will have to leave the ice and run on your skates several times?"

"No."

"Sir," said another from the back of the crowd. "Do you have any idea at all what it means to skate 200 kilometers on natural ice?"

"I guess I'll find out," I said.

"Yes," he said with a snicker, "I guess you will."

It seemed like only minutes later that I was being shaken from one dream into another. It was four o'clock in the morning, and I was in the home of a local insurance agent named Fokke (pronounced "fah-cur") de Boer. ("*Ja,* I know ze jokes about ze name.") As the full extent of the invasion of the town had become clear, the mayor of Leeuwarden asked the citizenry to open their homes to skaters, and more than 5,000 families had offered free beds to strangers.

Fokke and Elshe de Boer and their two teenage daughters were waiting down in the parlor. Elshe put several bars of chocolate into my pack, and the five of us went out the back door to get the family bicycles.

We rode very slowly through a fog that hung wet as a downpour, over cobblestones that were slick with a thin patina of ice. From the dark, I could see into the windows of parlor after parlor of small, ivy-covered houses. Inside, skaters rose like shadows from pallets on the floor, and in the orange light cast by paraffin fires or in the glow of televisions already broadcasting news of the race, I could see figures sitting and rubbing skate stones along their blades. People emerged from the houses and ran alongside the growing sea of bicycles, moving to the ice through a wet, long night.

—

I'd been skating in darkness for more than an hour before dawn finally lit the mist. I knew I was passing through farmland from the odors along the way, but it wasn't until the light rose that I saw sheep and cows and farmers standing motionless at the edges of their wet fields. I saw flat pastureland stretching back, deep green and endless, and as the mist began to hold a bit more light, I was presented with the sight of my first windmill. It was a simple one, with a small thatched base and four delicate canvas-covered blades, but it was there.

"Windmill," I breathed at a tall skater who'd come up alongside me.

He looked up at the windmill for quite a while as we drew even with it. "*Ja,* a windmill," he said. He clasped his hands high behind his back and leaned forward. Then he moved 15 yards ahead of me with one deep, formalist stride.

All around me skaters seemed to be moving to the same cadent dirge. There were long, snaking lines of skaters from the same village or town, all of them skating in a careful, even rhythm, their bodies so close behind one another that they could have rested their chins on each other's backs.

I watched hundreds of the finest skaters I'd ever seen pass me by, and their steady strides now seemed particularly amazing. In the soft light, I could see why I'd had to keep my knees bent like a skier traversing a mogul field during the hour in the dark. The surface of the ice was deeply rutted with cracks two and three inches wide, and with every lateral movement across the width of the canal, the ice seemed to be of completely different consistencies. There were places where small ice floes had risen and frozen, leaving a two-inch-high ridge along the surface, and there were deep holes.

Through conversations with several racers, I learned that the blackest ice would be the smoothest for another hour or so; then the rising temperature would make it slow. The alternative was white ice, which was full of snow and frozen pockets where a misplaced blade could crash through up to the boot. I was told to pay particular attention to the broad central crack zigzagging the length of the canal because many people break their ankles wedging a skate in the crack and having their bodies continue past it.

By the time we passed the cheering, singing crowds in the little village of Scharnegoutum, my pace had fallen off considerably. Eventually a barrel-chested, middle-aged man skated up next to me, and when we realized we were moving at a similar pace, we began to chat. His name was Hans Christian Schwenck, and he'd come up from The Hague for the event.

"What wonderful ice," he said. "A hint of spring in the air and wonderful ice."

I asked him if he wasn't soaked to the bone from the heavy fog, as I was.

"Of course," he said, glancing at me quizzically.

As we skated under bridges and across small lakes, he began to recall past races. In 1940, he said, the five leaders of the race clasped hands at the finish line and came across together, an act since banned from the competition.

We passed a group of farmers standing silently near a tractor, and Hans said, "Standing there so still like that, it reminds me of the race in '42. The German troops stood along the banks and just stared at us. The ice was good that year too—stone hard and black as pitch. Almost everyone in the race registered under a false name. It was quite a reunion for the underground."

"You skated in '42?"

"*Ja*. And '41."

"How old are you?"

"I'm 63," Hans answered, then excused himself and picked up his pace.

Unlike almost every sport that involves strength and coordination, the best long-distance skaters are not young. A few weeks before I arrived in Holland, a 60-year-old marathon skater had placed third in a 150-kilometer race. The man who'd won the 1933 Elfstedentocht had gone on to set a world record for 200 kilometers while in his mid-sixties and held it for several years. Jan Kruithof is 48 years old, Crazy Dries is about to turn 40, and all but a few of the best marathoners are over 35. Kruithof said he felt he'd peaked at 43—after 40 years on ice. The idea of some 19-year-old sprinter having the endurance and will to win a 200-kilometer event amused the mature skaters.

—

At the outskirts of the medieval, brownstone village of Sneek (pronounced "Snake"), I began to see people pointing at my skates and calling out my name. I had apparently become a minor celebrity in Holland, not so much because I was the first American, but because I was the first skater foolish enough to try the race on *ijshockeyschaaten*. A photograph of the American wearing an inane grin and holding his hockey skates in the air appeared on the front page of the sports section of the country's biggest newspaper the morning of the race and hit the stands by the time I hit Sneek.

I was a skating fool in Sneek. I could dance over the widening puddles and do sidesteps and crossovers around the great gulfs in the ice as only a wearer of short blades can. I was particularly skilled at the dreaded *klunen* that began in Sneek, those places where we had to climb off the canal, run through town over rugs and hay bales, and then climb back down to the ice. Compared to the 16,122 others who had to shuffle along on their long touring blades, I flew through these portages.

The caption under my photograph in the morning paper contended that I "had every confidence in my ice hockey skates," but a few miles past the beautiful 700-year-old village of Ijlst, the statement began to strike me as one of the least intelligent assertions ever offered in print. My skates were clearly designed for something other than skating across the Netherlands. They were made for dodging puddles and body checks, for controlled, short bursts of speed, and neat, quick turns. As I observed another thousand or so skaters passing me, I became aware that I was taking at least three strides to every one of theirs. The blades of the skates flying by me were even longer than the speed skates worn by sprinters, the boots low to the blade to facilitate the classic skater's pose: head low, hands fixed behind the back. The Dutchmen couldn't have made the most obtuse turns if their lives depended on it, but they could go straight like nothing I'd ever seen. I felt as if I were riding a tricycle among ten-speed racers.

My lower back was completely tied in knots, and my knees were so battered from absorbing the constant shock of rough ice that I felt as if I'd been kneecapped. My layers of clothes had been wet and partially frozen since long before dawn, but now they felt as heavy as chain mail, and I longed for one of those nifty polypropylene skating suits.

I'd also discovered why everyone else in the race looked as if they were wearing catcher's mitts on their knees. Despite the long skate blades, all around me people were taking painful falls; some of them looked as if they'd just skated off a ski jump, bodies arching through the damp air and landing in heaps. Others fell from the hay bales during the *klunen* and those behind piled on top. Twice, I saw skaters go down and take a whole club along with them. The fallen would crawl to the reeds at the edge of the canal and try to suck some air back into their lungs, but no matter how badly they seemed to be hurt, they always got up and continued.

I considered the knifelike projections protruding from the ice and decided that I simply would not fall down. So in my constant effort to yank my skates out of holes and maintain my balance, I'd managed to pull most of the muscles along my upper back by the time I skated onto the huge, dreaded inland lake called Slotenmeer.

A white cloud had descended onto the lake, and it was so dense that after a few strides the shoreline disappeared. With huge stumps and treetops rising through the ice, Slotenmeer looked like the proverbial haunted forest of no return. The surface of the windswept ice was as pocked as the surface of the moon, and it was all I could do to keep my balance. At one point I completely lost the *schaats-route* and came face to face with a stream of skaters who had already rounded the village of Sloten on the other side of the lake and were heading back the other way.

By the time I found the route again, I had seen my eventual fate. I was certain I would lose strength, take one of the terrifying falls occurring all around me, and die. There would be no story in America about my race, but I would probably make the Dutch papers for the second day in a row.

At the far end of the lake, the mist broke briefly, and I saw the magnificent windmill of Sloten rise like an apparition on a promontory on the other side of the cloud. It was the biggest, most beautiful windmill I'd ever seen. Beneath it a huge circus calliope was filling the distance with music, and I could see people standing along the narrow canal, dancing to the tunes. Other racers had been stopping along the way at little stands selling soup and hot chocolate, but I hadn't dared slow down, even at the stamping points. I had skated close to 30 miles, and my map indicated the next town was 15 miles away. For quite a while my head had been pounding with a pain I'd diagnosed as jet lag, but I didn't want to stop. Still, how could I just skate past this most glorious of windmills?

I hoisted myself up onto a retaining wall and dangled my legs over the side. As I felt my clothes begin to freeze around me, I stared up at the majestic windmill until I noticed spectators on the other side of the canal pointing at my skates and waving. Soon I was surrounded by people asking me for . . . my autograph.

Eventually somebody talked me into taking off my skates for a while and coming up to a thatch-roofed inn for a bowl of soup. The inn was full of warmth and good cheer, and inside, Dutchmen with long, curving pipes watched the A-class racers fly past one of the 40 television cameras spaced along the route.

I sat at a table with a group of policemen and numerous Dutch tourists who recognized me. One man contended with certitude that a visiting Canadian had once unofficially attempted the Elfstedentocht on hockey skates, but he'd been dragged from the course, exhausted, before he had reached the first village. This overwhelmed me with pleasure—especially since I realized I had to immediately put my head down on the table next to my soup and go to sleep.

I remember several bus rides after I called it quits in Sloten and at least one train ride back to Leeuwarden and the finish line, but I don't remember getting on or off any of them.

———

As darkness fell over the course again, thousands of people were still racing. Bands played late into the night for them, and spectators stood in the cold singing them songs. Sometimes, skaters would stop and stand in front of a crowd with their hands raised in the air, or even pause for a minute to dance with the spectators.

Hours earlier, a young farmer named Evert van Benthem had won the race in just 6 hours, 46 minutes, breaking the old record by 49 minutes. The next three finishers, who'd paced Evert all day, crossed the finish line so close behind him that all four shared the same time.

The sun never appeared to light the day, but the temperature rose enough that by nightfall the skaters were traveling through water above their ankles. At the finish line, I saw exhausted skaters fall to their knees to kiss the ice, then trudge back into the Frieslandhal in Leeuwarden to find much of the skin gone from their feet. Some of them sat in chairs, holding bright bouquets and looking like corpses; others sifted through the thousands of shoes that had been piled on the bank of the canal that morning.

For hours, I watched skaters limp into the hall. Alongside me was Gunther Meyer, a pleasant man in his fifties who was an MP with the Royal Dutch Air Force.

"The ice was really something today, wasn't it?" I said to Gunther Meyer.

"It certainly was," he said. "Best ice I've skated on in years."

Gunther had readied himself for the race by double-timing 40 miles a week with a 25-pound pack on his back because, as he said, "People with easy lives can't do things like this. And only Dutchmen can really race the Elfstedentocht"—a sentiment I'd come to share.

It seemed like everyone in Friesland had come to the great hall by early evening, easily 20,000 people dancing to an oompah band and waiting anxiously for their friends and relatives to appear. By the time the first 12 race finishers had mounted a platform at one end of the Frieslandhal, the huge crowd was singing along with the band. The governor of the province gave a short speech in Fries, and the crowd went crazy with appreciation. Evert van Benthem told the crowd he was thankful for his victory and for the wonderful condition of the ice. He said later that he'd been out of training until just before the race because he had purchased some new cows for his 17th-century farm.

J. R. Kruithof had come in 13th, nine minutes behind the winner, but as he greeted the hysteria his name induced throughout the hall, he seemed so genuinely moved that it didn't seem to matter that he'd lost a race he'd been training for every day for 22 years. Then he and a group of skaters—including Crazy Dries, who'd come in tenth—hoisted van Benthem above their heads as the crowd screamed its approval.

A reporter pulled me from the throng and asked how I felt about having to drop out of the race and not receive the cross that more than 13,000 skaters would be awarded. I told the reporter he didn't understand. I said that just a few hours ago I had skated out of a white cloud and found myself in front of the windmill of Sloten, and people had called out my name . . .

Then the crowd rose to an astonishing, keening pitch that drowned us out.

There was more collective passion in that provincial hall than is contained in a decade's worth of Superbowls. The outpouring I wit-

nessed in the Frieslandhal that night was the result of an entire nation waiting a generation so that 16,000 Dutch men and women
could show that they were skilled enough and tough enough to skate
124 miles in a single day. The interminable wait for ice in Friesland
had all of the elements of an ancient people waiting for a comet,
until the endless ribbons of water comprising 14,000 acres of Friesland had finally frozen and stitched the landscape into a whole, so
that Dutchmen could show the world what ice skating really ought
to be.

Outside, November 1985

PART II

AMERICA

THE BOYS IN THE PITS

Early in the morning, Harry Grace hobbled painfully across the floor of the Chicago Mercantile Exchange toward the charts on the east wall of the temple of free enterprise. He pressed his spasmodic lower back as he pointed to a thin black line that documented two things: the recent vicissitudes in the price of the $1-million lots of U.S. Treasury bill futures that Harry trades, and the recent history of Harry's personal health and well-being. An extra piece of graph paper was pasted below one segment of the chart to accommodate the T-bills' violent dip to the floor that began in November 1979. "My ulcer," Harry said. Then the 28-year-old commodities futures trader turned carefully toward his T-bill pit and moved to its wooden steps like a man three times his age, one pain clutched firmly in each hand. Like many floor traders, Harry planned to spend the afternoon in a health-club sauna recovering from his working day; but first he had to make it through four hours of screaming, anxious bobbing and weaving, and the making and losing of much money, until the gong at 1:40 P.M. would allow him to stagger away.

Four thousand people wearing their colors stood around Harry in the huge, windowless space. The shapeless coats worn at the Merc are of peculiarly bright, technological colors: lemon-yellow for the runners; sky-blue for the Exchange's employees (the referees); and cherry-red for the floor traders themselves ("the players," "the boys"). With its general aura of nonskid ultramodernity, the floor of the Exchange looked as if a factoryful of German computer makers had been hustled into the main lobby of the Frankfurt airport and were waiting for some very bad news. Each trader appeared to be restraining his own case of financial panic; each toed his own private line. Some stroked their neckties—ties that bore dollar signs, and ties that bore bulls and bears with dollar signs branded on their flanks. Some argued about yesterday's trades; some talked soothingly to themselves; and some just looked scared. Behind the octagonal hog pit, a hog man who is known to perspire incessantly from the moment he sets foot on the Exchange floor was sweating like—well, he was soaking wet.

Harry waved to other traders and inquired as to their injuries. "How's the leg, Jim?" he said to a trader near the Canadian-dollar pit. Jim, like many young floor traders, has varicose veins.

"Eh," Jim said, shrugging. "How's the back, Harry?"

"How's the gut, Sam?" another floor trader near the gold pit inquired of a colleague.

The work had taken an evident physical toll on even the youngest of the commodities traders, many of whom were under 25. Prematurely salt-and-pepper hair fell to varying lengths over the often tanned but always strained faces.

Down the street at the mighty Chicago Board of Trade, the only futures exchange in the world larger than the Chicago Merc, traders have dropped dead right in the wheat pit. A few years ago a man was felled by a heart attack in the Board of Trade soybean pit three minutes before the opening gong. "He was on the floor, and his face was blue," a yellow-jacketed pit clerk remembered, "but they didn't delay the opening. Hell, no. The runners just stepped over him."

At precisely 8 A.M., the gong sounded the beginning of T-bill futures trading. Suddenly the towering east wall of what the industry's boosters call "the last breath of capitalism"—or, as all the commodities boys like to say, "the last frontier"—began to undulate with spinning numerals like an electric flight-departure board gone berserk. Men with public-address systems for voices bellowed promises for the future at one another, craning their necks unnaturally as they tried to watch the boards flash new numbers. All of them leaned into the press of the pit with their heads tilted toward the ceiling, like tired swimmers, like dogs baying at the moon.

A few minutes later the foreign-currency pits of the burgeoning IMM—the International Monetary Market, a recent addition to the Merc—kicked into gear, and the trading floor became an effluvium of clashing colors, flailing arms, screams, and horrible facial expressions. Traders and runners seemed to fall down the three steps into their pits and then fall back up again. Red-faced traders performed a gesture in which both hands flew from behind their ears as if to hurl their heads into the pit. They spun from one side of the pit to the other; they bumped and pushed, turning mechanically on their heels and dancing back to deposit their chins in other traders' faces and wail numbers up into their noses.

This is the daily ritual of people who believe that they are the last true individualists in America because they have what it takes to stand alone. Virtually unencumbered by government regulations, monopolistic power, fancy academic degrees, or even the requirements of fundamental human civility, a man—and men is what an estimated 97 percent of commodities traders are—can make a clean killing of mammoth proportions. He can climb into the trading pits in Chicago and stare into another's eyes, and by virtue of the superior tuning of the calculator that all good traders carry in their heads—simply because at that moment his aggression is a little more closely attuned to the milliticks of the market—he can wipe the imported-German-airport floor with another trader's children's futures. In an ill-timed blink of an eye, a trader can blunder away the house on the lake, the country-club membership, and the Mercedes. A head cold, a hangover, or even a stutter, coupled with a fleeting warp in the market, and "Boom!" as one trader puts it, "your kids don't go to college."

"There are no friends in the pit," a gold trader says grimly. "And you can quote me. You do not take prisoners in here."

The commodities market is, as they *always* say, the last frontier, and often the reaction to its quick-draw deaths is tears. Almost every trader volunteers in the course of conversation a tale of men failing so completely—in full view of the others in the pit—that they simply begin to cry. "Yeah, just the other day," a bearded trader said to me, "this guy's blubberin' and cryin' and gettin' down in front of me on his knees beggin' me for twenty grand. It was really pitiful."

Harry Grace shed tears once in his T-bill pit, but that was because another trader had stabbed him in the right cheek with one of the shiny black pencils they fling around like sabers. Harry's rage was so great that one old-timer on the floor could tell that he was "off." When you're off, you shoot wildly and you lose it; so, for Harry's own good, the trader escorted him off the floor for the day.

———

Several basic facts contribute to the throbbing intensity of the commodities trade. For one thing, some 80 percent of those who trade in futures will lose their money. That's point one. Then there is the phenomenon of leverage. Commodities speculation is considered the one last method this side of bank robbery by which you can quickly accumulate important amounts of money without having much to start out with, and the reason is that you have to put hardly anything on the table to get into the game. *But* if the price goes the wrong way, you have to come up with the difference immediately; and if it goes the wrong way the next day, you have to fork out again. Since most trades involve large numbers of T-bill contracts, vaultfuls of silver, or carloads of hogs, a bad day of trading often results in a phone call that evening informing you of the day's debts in six, seven, eight, or (if you are really unlucky) nine, or even (if you are the Hunt brothers of Dallas, Texas) ten figures. If you can't meet the margin call quickly, they'll sell your valuable trading seat, along with your boat, car, gold neck chains, and anything else you have, and thus deal you out of the great big game forever.

—

Every morning at 9:05, a deafening roar emanates from the middle of the floor as the boys in the cattle pit begin to adjust the price of next year's steaks by buying and selling hundreds and thousands of steers that haven't even been conceived yet. Last year the cattle-pit trades in soon-to-be steers totaled nearly a million more than the entire number of transactions on the Chicago exchanges in 1976.

A chief beneficiary of the escalation of trading in live cattle is another kid named Harry. This morning he stood in his favorite corner of the pit, waving a huge fistful of the customer orders called decks. Thirty-two-year-old Harry "the Hat" Lowrance is one of the hip young superstars who have flocked to the Chicago exchanges during the past few years. Harry the Hat has one of the biggest decks in Chicago, and Harry gives great, great fills. In other words, when Harry buys and sells for his customers, he gets the best prices around. The orders in Harry's deck make him much more money in a year than the President of the United States gets, and the size of his deck makes him all but a god to the new breed of traders.

When Harry finishes for the day, he collapses into a lengthy burgundy limousine (license plate: HAT). His chauffeur drives him to his huge old mansion on the shore of Lake Michigan, where he sits in his glass-enclosed sauna and stares out over the heartland sea that used to bring the boats that brought the grain that led the farmers and millers to form an exchange, which allowed Harry the Hat, a poor kid from Chicago, to accumulate so much money that he can sit in a glass sauna and watch the lake freeze over and thaw out again for the rest of his life if he wants to. The floors in Harry's living room are beveled glass mirrors, and the walls are covered with blue quilted wool adorned with gold and silver leaf. Harry has his own soda fountain, and in the bathrooms are showers with nozzles that shoot you everywhere.

Like the gunfighters and athletes that they are, floor traders acquire nicknames that attend their legends. Harry's is derived from his trading badge, HAT. The badges are the letters on the traders' jerseys ("Do you know CALM?" SLEW will say to CAL). The day I observed Harry the Hat in action, I also watched OZ and WHAM and MOB and MAD prance through the pits like dervishes trading one another's futures.

Swirling around Harry the Hat that day, feeding off his giant deck, was a cattle trader in a monogrammed pink trading jacket with white piping. His entire head had turned deep purple and clashed with his outfit. Harry was also involved in a long series of rapid trades with a very hot 31-year-old trader named Alan Young, a kid from the South Side of Chicago and a former Cook County state's attorney. Harry also trades with a former doctor, a few former professors, lots of former lawyers, and even a former florist who is said to have the most violent temper in the pits.

Next door in the pork-belly pit, the old-boys' club at the Merc, the belly traders were beginning to get cranked up. The belly boys are said to "keep a girl upstairs" for their passing pleasure. A famous belly tale is the legend of the "$100,000 head": A trader holding a large position thought the daily down-limit fluctuation had bottomed, so he went upstairs with the legendary lady of the bellies. When he came back down, the story goes, he found that his market positions had improved by $100,000. Such is pit humor.

——

On the other side of the cattle pit is the live-hog pit. There I watched a 32-year-old trader with long hair and a beard, like an old Zap Comix character, as he waited, he said, "for my psyche to come alive"—which occurs only when he hears the hog gong. His success in the pits has allowed him to purchase a many-bedroomed mansion in a suburb just north of Harry the Hat's house. Another of the hog traders used to be a Chicago policeman, one of the cops involved in the famous raid on the Chicago Black Panther headquarters in 1969, when the Panther leader Fred Hampton was killed. "He's all right in the pits, you know," one colleague says of the ex-policeman, "but you can sort of tell he's been awful mean in his time and could be that way again if he wanted to."

There are a number of ex–Chicago policemen in the pits, most of whom are there—directly or indirectly—because of one Eugene Cashman, a cop who used to walk the beat around the Board of Trade building in the 1950s, until he decided to go inside and trade. Cashman did well; he caught the '73 soybean market and is now estimated to have made somewhere between $50 million and $80 million.

Another ex-cop who trades over at the Board of Trade is considered one of the hottest kids on the floor. (They are all kids; 22-year-olds refer to 45-year-old veterans as kids.) A young millionaire and man-about-town commodities trader I'll call Billy Bowman originally talked him into leaving his beat to "come on down" to the fast lane. Later, Billy started hitting the white powder pretty hard during trading hours, and then, very quickly, Billy lost it. He "tapped out," as they say of their casualties. He lost his $3 million a lot quicker than he had made it; he lost his house; he lost his wife, who divorced him; and then, his old friends confirm, Billy even lost his mind and entered an institution for a couple of months.

Of all the accoutrements of wealth associated with the Chicago trade in commodities futures—the mansions, the Rolls-Royces, the Rush Street ladies—the salient emblem in recent years has been cocaine. In 1979, with this fact in mind, federal Drug Enforcement Administration agents stormed onto the floor of the Chicago Options Exchange (located above the Board of Trade) and dragged ten people, including three red-coated traders, off the floor and into paddy wagons for possession and trafficking. But the trade continues, most of it conducted by the young runners and clerks.

The runners stand at the traders' elbows, scream like them, watch their moves, talk in their tribal language, and receive their occasional abuse. They move rapidly across the crowded floor, taking shoulder blocks and illegal clips, because 15 seconds can cost a runner's boss a fortune. All this for lower weekly wages than any half-decent trader can make in a minute. A lot of the runners say they've seen the future down on the floor, and a few of them, at age 17, are already saving their money for down payments on the tremendous loans they will need to buy a $250,000 IMM seat or a $330,000 badge at the Board of Trade.

In workingmen's corners of Chicago, cops and sons of cops don't hear much about Billy Bowman's cocaine downfall; they just hear about Officer Cashman. And in the North Chicago high schools they hear tales of Harry the Hat Lowrance. Because Horatio Alger still walks the streets of Chicago, Illinois. Given a quick mind, a strong voice, the ability to sustain a few setbacks, some financial backing, and a compulsive sense of order, a kid can climb down into the pits along with the kinds of cops who used to beat up long-haired kids and the kinds of kids who used to get beaten—and shoot it out for real.

—

I was standing near the currency pits at the Merc one morning when I was shocked to see Joe Mooney in Swiss francs. Back when we'd studied European economies together in London, Joe was known for his tweedy garb and for the powerful mind that allowed him to easily envisage complicated economic configurations. Confused students used to flock to Joe rather than go to the professors for help. For a moment he looked just as I remembered him. Then his moustache twitched, his eyes opened wide, and he exploded onto his toes and bellowed, "Twenty on ten!"

Back in Arizona, Joe's mother wishes he had a more secure job, but Joe says that he's secure in his decision to scream intelligently for a living. In exchange for a secretary, profit-sharing plans, pensions, stock options, three-piece suits, and a few other perks of the main line, Joe makes $2,000 or $3,000 on an average day of trading (his best day netted around $25,000, and his worst cost him $45,000). He made around $6,000 the day I peered over his shoulder. He goes home at 1:30 in the afternoon. As a scalper and spreader, Joe holds speculative positions for no longer than seconds or minutes. He makes money on tiny market swings—$1,000 here, $600 there. Scalpers and big position traders share the highest status on the floor because they trade their own accounts, working alone and gaining and losing their own money.

This is not to say that floor brokers like Harry Grace and Harry the Hat Lowrance don't take risks. When a broker filling a customer's order makes a big mistake, he pays in blood. Just before I arrived in Chicago, a broker in the silver pit at the Board oversold 14 silver contracts by mistake. Though he realized his error in ten seconds, the market was flying that day and it cost him $190,000 of his own money to make things right.

———

If you lose it, you "take a very heavy hit," in the colorful lingo of the trade. You "give it back," "suck some gas." You go "in the dinger" or "underwater," or you get "blown out." When you see a winning position falling away, you dive into the pit and "puke out" your position. You try to "get a leg up" when you are "short the wings" on a "butterfly spread." You can "goose" a market, "shock" a market, "make" a market, "ride" a market, "bleed" a market, and even "fight" a market; but if you fight it, brother, you will lose.

Nothing changes a market—making and breaking fortunes in the process—like new information. There is a genre of floor traders known as machine men. The machine men stand in front of the computer screens or ticker-tape machines, trying to make sense of the outside world faster than the guys 30 feet away in the pit. They watch the electronic price boards, the stock-market tapes, and the other commodity exchanges' prices, as well as the news wires. Then they lumber maniacally toward the pit, mouths agape with the horror of their new information.

Facts fall onto the floor of a commodities exchange like tomatoes into a Cuisinart. According to the news on the Chicago trading floors, the hostages in Iran have been released four times and shot five; the Russians have invaded Iran twice; the Chinese have invaded Afghanistan to get at the Russians; the Syrians have invaded Israel; Khomeini has been shot twice and has twice died of natural causes; and King Khalid of Saudi Arabia's heart has finally given out. Poor Marshal Tito suffered death no fewer than 12 times before finding peace.

One day, the sad news that a female runner had been murdered in the elevator of her apartment building arrived at one end of the Merc. It emerged at the other end of the floor as the "fact" that Federal Reserve Board chairman Paul Volcker had just had a heart attack and had died in the elevator of the Chicago Mercantile Exchange; and the markets wheeled and gyrated people's savings accounts away in response.

Most traders make fun of the machine men because, they say, those boys lack the subtle sensitivity required in the current crazy markets. The best and most successful traders say that their secret is "feel" (about 80 percent of them), technique (about 12 percent), or the fundamentals of supply and demand (about 4 percent). Various other factors, such as noise level, hunches, fate, and God's will, constitute the methodologies of the rest.

The technical trader, or chart trader, believes in and studies only the market itself. He looks for historical patterns and relationships between prices to find a trend. His is a world of random walk, computerized odds, and n-game theory, and he spends nights and weekends making new charts.

The fundamentalist, who believes in economic functions like supply and demand and in notions like cause and effect—who thinks that a bumper crop ought to press the price down—is part of a peripheral minority in a deranged market system whose old rules have just plain stopped working.

The lofty old justifications for men's living and working amid such anarchy are latter-day Mandevillian concoctions that speak of all the public good born of private avarice. The traders, by setting a price for the producers and providing liquidity, allow farmers, meat packers, or photographic companies that need silver to insure against, or hedge, the future's uncertainty. Companies can hedge changes in the interest rate on the T-bill or other financial markets, and many of them do. But even hedgers are speculating these days, because the risk factor has ballooned beyond anyone's expectations.

The commodities exchanges have been around for more than a century in this country, and for most of that time the world of main-line high finance has viewed them as a faintly seedy alternative. But things have changed. Despite the growing risk, people who used to see banks as too chancy a place to park their funds are now taking their money into the pits—to boys who are perfectly willing to shoulder risk and to trade other people's futures for their own reward.

—

A continual source of controversy is the question of how much chance can be involved in a risk–reward relationship like the modern commodities futures trade before it becomes gambling. Earlier in the century, some states had strict laws that outlawed futures contracts; but the courts eventually ruled that exchanges were not gambling dens, because a person who buys a contract can theoretically get delivery of the real commodity. Gambling, apologists say, serves no social purpose, while futures markets have helped producers share their risks with others ever since the *cho-ai-mai* market opened up in Japan in the 17th century. But nobody can remember a risk factor comparable to that of the last two years in Chicago.

"These young people down here now, they're taking a terrible, terrible risk," says Mike Weinberg. At 80, Weinberg is a second-generation commodities trader. His father was a charter member of the Chicago Merc, and out of habit Weinberg still arrives at the Merc at 6 A.M. In the old days, he spent the early-morning hours before trading started loading real commodities—eggs and butter—onto real trucks from real Chicago warehouses.

Weinberg stopped trading in the pits ten years ago, because of the increasing violence of the younger men. "They knocked me down, knocked off my glasses, and stepped all over me. But, you know, it's easier to find my car downstairs in the garage now. These young people—if they're right—they buy Mercedes-Benzes and Rolls-Royces and houses for $300,000 up in Highland Park. These young kids . . . I mean, you just can't believe it."

By the sheer force of the wealth they have accumulated in recent years, the commodities boys have muscled their influence into all corners of the city. They have risen up as a coherent subculture, much like the late-19th-century immigrant industrialists. They are no longer viewed as parasites living off the real work of stacking wheat and butchering hogs for the world. Power has come to the great halls of speculation that used to fit into the pores of Chicago's "real" business like so much grit. The city's banks now contain the largest pool of speculative capital in the world, larger than that in the "paper cities" of London and New York.

The Chicago White Sox baseball team is controlled by a consortium of Board of Trade members, and the local professional soccer team is solely owned by Lee Stern, one of the city's major grain traders. South of the ballfield, at the prestigious University of Chicago Business School, a $500,000 grant from the Chicago exchanges is helping to endow a new Futures Industry Study Center. At Faces, Chicago's trendiest disco, the best pickup procedure any young banker or CPA can employ is to answer the inevitable "Whadda ya do?" with a nonchalant "Oh, I'm down in the bean pit at the Board."

—

The Board of Trade looks like the granddaddy that it is. It is the fine old Wrigley Field to the upstart Merc's Astrodome. There is a grim grade-school dullness to the tiled floor, and the trading coats worn in the huge old wheat pit are faded. There is much less long hair, and many of the men speak with broad Irish accents that pour unceasingly from their ruddy Irish mugs. In contrast to the Merc, where the odors of anxiety are efficiently sucked away by an advanced ventilation system, you can still smell the 132-year-old history of carnage and elation at the Board. They used to keep piles of real corn and wheat on sample tables back in the days when the traders could tell good grain from bad, back before the hip young kids who couldn't separate the wheat from the chaff came on down.

The runners seem older at the Board, especially the women.

Some of these arrive for work in fur coats and appear to take part in a good deal of playful grabbing with the even older traders. The business is coordinated by, and dependent on, women's work, but the status of women at the Board has advanced little since 1969, when they were first allowed on the floor. I heard one grudging approbation for the few women who now trade their own accounts: a trader's contention that "a few of these gals are a lot less emotional than the men."

The machismo of the commodities world is transcended only by the towering levels of its athleticism. Many traders seem obsessed by athletics. One corner of the wheat pit at the Board is filled with former Chicago professional athletes trading their own accounts. Ex–Chicago Cubs Glen Beckert and George Altman are both successful traders. Former Chicago Bears defensive tackle George Seal is a formidable pit adversary and a hot property on the racquetball courts, where many traders continue combat after closing.

I watched a former ranked Colorado State handball player named Chuck Wafer trade fortunes' worth of soybeans. In the bean pit they call Chuck Wafer the Ice Man. He is a tall, muscular fellow whose clear green eyes appear to cover the tote boards without his having to turn his head.

Chuck says that it is the ice, the self-control, that has seen him through the rough times—such as the year he didn't make a dime. (Well, he made $100,000, but relatively speaking the year was a washout.)

"I walked scared," Chuck said after his trading day had ended. "Anytime you start relaxing, they get you. When you get cocky, or you think you're better than you are, or you're belligerent . . . they get you."

The best thing a big speculator can have is discipline. The traders all talk about discipline because it is the only thing that can tame the tapeworm that makes someone become a commodities trader in the first place. The incredible slew of anxieties on the trading floor is the result less of overt greed or fear than of the tension of holding back, of trying to gain some control over the deep conviction that the great moment traders all know is inside them will finally be theirs.

The worst thing a trader can have is an "attitude." An attitude is a perfervid belief about the direction of the market upon which a speculator is willing to stake his family's livelihood. A trader I'll call Max has had more attitudes than all but a few active traders, and thus making and losing multimillion-dollar fortunes has become his habit at a very young age. When we had lunch across the street from the Board, Max said, "I'm where a lot of the others have been." He was "in the dinger" around $1 million. He laughed when I asked him if he had ever made a million in six months, and said that he often makes a million in six days. He has stood in the pit and dropped fortunes of over $5 million many times, and each time he has plummeted to far below break-even. He once "gave back" $7 million in three tragic days of one-way attitudes.

Max was by far the best-read and most reflective trader I came across, and his cool was second only to that of Chuck Wafer, the Colorado Ice Man. Despite his losses, Max is respected as one of the most brilliant traders in the pits. "I am a speculator," Max said softly. "I speculate in futures. The numbers really aren't money, in many ways: they are gauges of how well I can do. What I'm after is the perfection of my craft, and so it has to mean nothing to lose $50,000. Just nothing." ("A speculator who dies rich," the old saying goes, "has died before his time.")

Max looked pained when I asked him what it was like to live inside the kind of bad days that would send most men out the window.

"Each time there's a little more grief," he said. "Each time I feel a lot older."

"Did you ever think of getting out when you were up?"

He looked incredulous and raised his voice. "I love this! I love this! It's what I *do*. The last thing in the world I would do is work outside for somebody else, for some corporation. I know that half the guys down there would rather die than give in to something like that."

Four weeks after we met, Max had more than recouped his million and was ready to fly again.

—

Who are these kids who bellow at one another on the last frontier? A lot of them, like Joe Mooney and Harry Grace, appear quite normal. Others seem obscenely selfish—the leeches that suck the blood of any generation's economy. But more than half the market's badges are held by true believers who have been on the floor for less than five years—baby-boom kids, many of whom used to have sincere doubts about the ethics of the profit motive. I met a 31-year-old gold arbitrager named Donnie James who had wandered the world for several years—all the way to Kabul, Afghanistan—before coming to the Merc. He had been a schoolteacher of handicapped kids and had also worked for the railroads. He has neat, longish hair, but he says it was once much longer.

"There are a lot of newborn attitudes down here, all right. A lot of reformed Grateful Dead fans who look at things differently now," he said. "Money does some funny things. . . . The business is really like a counterculture. It has its own language and its own hours. It is a romantic life, and it offers so many fantasies of what you can achieve for yourself. It's a financial Disneyland."

A young real estate agent who deals with many commodities boys describes them as "late-sixties dope dealers from college, corralled into one big room." In a sense, he has a point. The college marijuana distributor, circa 1969, can be said to have been taking a big risk and making a profit while providing a liquid market in the performance of a community service. He set a market price and used leverage to enhance his gains. To the uninitiated he was a menace to society, and every once in a while he got burned on a deal, or developed a one-way attitude and ended up being tapped out of the market by the local Mafia, the dean, or the police.

But the real estate agent is wrong in that, unlike the old drug salesmen, the young pit traders know nothing about the commodity itself. I went along the backs of a few of the pits and found that only half the people trading had actually seen, or knew the first thing about, the commodity they trade.

The more abstract the profit, the better it feels. The money these boys are after is "weird" money, easy money, quick, unstained money that is gained through no process of subservience, no devotion to any concept or individual beyond their own numbers and their own selves. They don't want empires; they want cash. Deep in the bourses of their hearts they think they're still rebels in the world of middle-class Protestant ethics, because theirs is the acquisitive drive of people who have come to believe that they *deserve* this money.

"Right here you have the logical conclusion of a generation that said things like 'We want it now' and 'We can have it all,' " one trader says. "But now it's '*I* can have it all, because the rest of you let me down.' Everybody down here is looking out only for himself."

"There are no social demands on you at all," explains a prominent floor manager who coordinates several brokers' floor trading. "There are no requirements of conformity. You must simply give good fills. You are beholden to nobody."

There's a term used on the floor to describe the actions of a trader who suddenly trades well beyond his usual limits; it's "flipping out." Many of the young traders appear to have flipped out into a parodic, all-consuming version of traditional business, much as others of their generation flipped out into health fanaticism or intense devotion to God. The pit is a secular temple in which the promise of true peace is always just beyond, in the ungraspable but tradable future.

The pit places a lucid template over things. In that world you are either "long" or "short" before you have to be anything else—like free or happy. You can occupy yourself with manageable fears of the IRS instead of fears of loneliness or rejection. The measure of how you're doing becomes completely numeric: you either win or lose.

As with religion, drugs, and, they say, killing people, the pit is hard to get away from once you've been there awhile. Max, the recidivist speculator, came into the business to make a million and get out; but somehow the exits keep moving away from him. For all their talk of personal freedom, the traders are slaves to the wavering whims of the market.

"Once it's in your arteries, you can't ever get away," says Donnie James, the former world traveler. "It's too big and too fast, and there's just too much money. I could never go back to a suit-and-tie life. I just couldn't. I'd have to hit the road again if I ever left the floor. I would be gone, man. That's for sure."

"I figure once you've been down here two years, you're not fit to do anything else at all," a trader named John Isham said, waiting for the gong at the Merc.

Sometimes they sound like General Patton: "It's economic warfare down there every day, but it's good warfare. It's damn good warfare." The traders are so totally immersed that they often feel at odds with the outside world. At night, for every Rush Street swinger there are three traders home alone with their charts. When they're in public without their colors, they look like football players in ill-fitting business suits or career soldiers in civvies.

—

Some economists and congressmen contend that the commodities market will soon drag the whole economy down into the pits. The financial panic that emanated from the silver pits in Chicago and New York last April—when the Hunt brothers' bad luck caused silver prices to fall 80 percent—spread with unprecedented speed to the stock markets and then into all the crannies of the Western world's economy. "For an hour and a half," one British expert wrote the next day, "it looked as if capitalism as we know it was to end."

The value of the promises made in the pits in 1979 exceeded this country's gross national product, and some argue cogently that commodities futures siphon needed money away from capital formation. Other analysts and would-be regulators of the industry say that futures trading is the destabilizing fuel of hyperinflation; still others insist that it provides a salubrious drag on inflationary trends. The fact is that nobody knows the economic ramifications of the action in the pits. It is clear only that the exchanges work best when the systems that govern the economies of the free world aren't working at all.

Assuredly, there will be many more futures in the future. New contracts for trading in the future of stock indexes such as the daily Dow Jones, or in the future prices of gasohol, diamonds, and oil, are being considered by the federal Commodity Futures Trading Commission, the agency that tries to control the business. In New York, traders began recently to speculate in wine vintages. At the grand old New York Stock Exchange, the brand-new New York Futures Exchange opened up last August to deal in a variety of currency and securities futures.

Back in Chicago they sneer at New York's fledgling efforts to cut in on their suzerainty. If the circulation of commodities is, as Marx said, the headwaters of capital, then capitalism flows pristine and swift in Chicago, Illinois, the last place where a man can live and die over money.

—

In the Merc cloakroom, after closing, wet red trading jackets were exchanged for ski vests and mink coats. The traders sat on benches with their hands dangling, like tired ballplayers. They talked market in hoarse voices for a while before retiring to saunas, bars, racket clubs, or their private Xanadus by the lake, or to their tiny offices, where traders often relive the "jiggles" of the day and thus live and die all over again.

As I was leaving the Exchange, a trader tapped my shoulder. "I was watching you at the closing today, and I know what you really felt: I know you felt it. I used to come down when I was little and just watch it from the window. I didn't even know what was going on, but I was so—amazed and happy. I saw you. . . . Nobody can know what it's like until they've stood up close to feel it. It's just so—so ferocious," he said in his ragged voice. "It's man against man."

Esquire, January 1981

THE ZEN MASTER OF MONEY

Al Frank emerged from his adobe-style high-desert home and moved toward his Toyota 4Runner with the careful, balletic steps of very big and gentle men. It was two hours before sunrise in the hills above Santa Fe, and a fierce full moon cast enough light so that he could read the front page of the 312th rendition of *The Prudent Speculator,* which Frank held between his teeth as he fumbled with his keys. Those who have bought and, very occasionally, sold the stocks Al Frank has bought and sold since he began sharing his insights with subscribers to his investment newsletter in 1977 now own common stock that has appreciated by nearly 800 percent over a period in which the Dow rose less than 250 percent. During the first decade of *The Prudent Speculator*'s existence—as wealth and fame accrued to Al Frank because of his special knack for culling undervalued stocks—the value of his pre–Crash of '87 portfolio rose at the startling compounded rate of 44 percent each year.

The prudent speculator himself is 62 now, and the Vandyke he sports is woven with gray. A mammoth Latin American cigar protruded like a beat cop's nightstick from an opening in his ski jacket.

Inside the Toyota, Al Frank began to talk slowly. Very slowly . . . slower, in fact, than anybody else in all of money world.

As we drove into the dark, chatting but more often sitting in silence because of the stunning distance between each of Al Frank's words, he said, "As . . . a child . . . I loved to get up at 4 A.M. . . . to accompany my uncle on his bakery route."

Then I waited. I have always wondered if perhaps Al hears voices, full conversations between each word he selects. "I think . . . I enjoyed . . . those mornings more than my uncle did," Al continued. "Because . . . one day . . . he . . . committed . . . suicide."

Back when Al Frank used to appear each week on the old Financial News Network, I would avidly await his mordant, preternaturally calm and Zen-like phrases—each juxtaposed against the razzmatazz, tell-ya-what-ah'm-a-gonna do, place-yer-bets, machine-gun syncopation of marketplace television reportage. Al once chose to appear on FNN wearing a toga. I also saw him on TV in a pith helmet and full jungle camouflage (as the "great stock hunter," he explained), and on two other occasions, around holiday season, Al swaddled his 275 pounds in a Santa Claus costume and spoke imperturbably of markets.

The jeep bounced along the washboard dirt road leading into downtown Santa Fe. The vermilion tips of the local chamiso plants glowed magically on either side of the road, across the hilly landscape. It was so early that the stoplights were still turned off in the old terminus of Santa Fe, where conquistadors once came in search of *El Dorado*—the Golden Man. The streets were empty of the props that enliven the endless dress-up party that is latter-day Santa Fe—the pearl-button cowboy shirts that turn retired dentists from Chicago into Roy or Kenny Rogers for the evening, the great turquoise ball 'n' chain ensembles that turn auto heiresses into Native American princesses. All the stress reduction centers, alternative book stores, massage universities, and life-change clinics that have turned Santa Fe into a New Age mecca were shuttered.

Al says he enjoys all the philosophical cogitating and all the quality-of-life improvement projects people take up in Santa Fe, a town he moved to from Southern California in 1991. "All theoretical concepts are grounded in practice," Al once wrote, "and most of my daily activities have a theoretical basis."

On the way to the printer, Al thought philosophically about money. "I would say I have a peculiar interest in money," he said with elaborate deliberation. "I like it, but not if I have to do . . . too much . . . for it. I don't want to work 12 hours a day for money, though I will work 12 hours a day on things that interest me."

Al Frank was once a Linotype operator and then a printshop owner in Northern California. He was a professional shill at the Flamingo Hotel in Las Vegas, and a down-and-out would-be writer living the vagabond life in a hut on an island in Spain. He was the publisher of *Jazz: A Quarterly of American Music* for a while, which he cofounded with the legendary music critic Ralph J. Gleason (who went on to help found *Rolling Stone* magazine). He was also a teaching associate in education at UCLA, has master's degrees in American studies and vocational rehabilitation, and his work toward a Ph.D. in philosophy of education emphasized linguistics and logic.

Al likes to tell people that he was just a typical working-class stiff, an adopted son of a Los Angeles tailor and his wife, and that he lived like an impoverished graduate student until he was 50. He wrote the first edition of what was then called *The Pinchpenny Speculator* at the age of 47, when his own portfolio contained just $8,007 in equity. But that portfolio began to grow like wildfire, and eventually Al Frank ascended through a pack of perhaps 1,000 investment-newsletter writers, who regularly hawk advice to some two million subscribers. He became one of a handful of "newsletter gurus" who rose to fame during the bull market of the 1980s because, for the few years preceding the precipitous downdraft of October 1987, it seemed that the best of these gurus could foretell the future.

———

The current marketplace in privately circulated investment prose includes newsletters that cost $75 a year and others that run close to

$600. There are newsletters that come with ancillary services such as panicky, middle-of-the-night phone calls to subscribers with buy and sell advice for the next morning. Newsletter writers are chartists, timers, switchers, bottom fishers, short sellers, sector specialists, options hounds, growth analysts, value investors, Fed watchers, specialists in mutual fund families, and computer-driven technicians. I used to get a very successful technical newsletter written by a former finance professor named Marty Zweig, and I'm not embarrassed to admit here that I could rarely figure out from the welter of figures in the letter whether Marty was telling me to buy or sell. There are astrologers who recommend stocks and commodity positions in investment newsletters. There are newsletter writers who are clearly lunatics but who truly believe the crazy advice they offer, and there are many more con men who don't believe a word of what's in their letters. A convicted grand larcenist named Christopher Lowe successfully argued his right to publish an investment newsletter—despite his track record—before the Supreme Court a few years back, and ever since then the SEC has registered and overseen only newsletter writers who are also investment advisors with individual clients.

The prose style of investment newsletters ranges from nonexistent to embarrassingly florid. Al Frank's letters stand out for their clarity and fluent prose. His writing displays hints of the beatific calm and languid thoughtfulness that characterize his personal style. Frank's 1990 book about his portfolio analysis method, *The Prudent Speculator: Al Frank on Investing,* renders amazingly simple the technical mechanics of the kind of stock selection process many professionals would prefer to keep murky and profitably intimidating. "Anyone should be able to understand investment principles," Al Frank says. "After all, it's not exactly Hegelian philosophy."

The Prudent Speculator abjures Hegelian discourse, but it does occasionally touch upon Taoism, the interplay of investing and psychology, and the vagaries of semantics. Frank refuses to "personify" the stock market ("The market is not alive. It does not give and take away"), and he will not make a distinction between investment and speculation.

"The market is an organizing principle that causes people to do amazing things, both rational and irrational," Al said as we again drove through empty Santa Fe. "Successful speculating is more a matter of character than mathematics, analysis, or luck," he has counseled his readers. "A rich and full life awaits the speculator who recognizes the nature of things and applies himself to them in a modest and intelligent manner."

"I still have certain flaws of character," Al said as we returned to his skylit Saltillo-tiled home, still before sunrise but minutes before the opening bell in New York. As soon as he can discern these flaws, Al will undoubtedly inventory them for his readers and anyone else who asks. Al Frank will tell you about his marriages (three), how much he weighs, about his sex life, about how much money he has, and how much money he makes. He will show you his tax returns and his buy and sell slips if you like. Whereas most newsletter writers publish hypothetical model portfolios, Frank prints his actual, personal portfolio in *The Prudent Speculator*. If Al needs to borrow on margin to abet his move to Santa Fe or to finance his daughter's wedding, his readers know about it. If the 51 stocks he picked at the end of 1990 have appreciated by 66.4 percent through October 1992, while the general market measured by the Dow has gone up only 22.5 percent, Al will be sure to tell you first about the character flaws that led him to choose two companies—Cascade International and HomeFed—that have gone out of business and off the board. And you immediately like Al Frank because of all of this. You trust that this is a man who simply cannot lie.

—

Back at his desk at sunrise, I watched Frank download data jacked up and over the Rockies by John Buckingham, the research director for *The Prudent Speculator* back in the newsletter's headquarters in Santa Monica.

The top of the desk, the bookshelves, and various tables in Al Frank's home office were heaped with bags full of vitamins, herbal pellets, and all sorts of crumbled leaves and powders that had been prescribed by a local practitioner of Indian Ayurvedic medicine Al met. There were poetry books, books of quotations, books about the stock market, New Age books by Santa Fe locals, and much older tracts by various ancient mystics and philosophers. Copies of the *I Ching* sat on top of copies of *Barron's,* and several dozen editions of competing investment newsletters were scattered about. There were humidors, loose cigars, a history of other people's business cards, credit cards, flashlights, a Weight Watchers scale, and computer-printout analyses of stocks Al Frank expects to double in price over the next three years. And there was an extra large Gun Muffler head-set of the sort seen on airport runways that Al clamps on his head when his wife, Vicki, is talking on the phone or watching TV.

Al drew forth a remote-control clicker from the desktop swirl and pointed it at a big Mitsubishi television facing his desk. Bill Griffith, his old friend from FNN days, came into focus on CNBC. Bill was looking dour because of the failure of the Fed to lower interest rates and the failure of the Germans to lower their rates. There would surely be a big sell-off at the opening on faraway Wall Street.

Within minutes the stock and bond markets were in precipitous decline. Just after 9 A.M. in Santa Fe, the Dow was off more than 100 points.

"Waterfall . . . sell-off," said Al Frank, still calm and still above the fray. But then, after the old prudent speculator drew in a very long and very slow breath, he whispered, "Oh, damn."

On his big and open face, I could see worry and a wince of pain.

—

It was a similar moment, one devoid of the tranquility Al Frank seeks to bring to his and other people's lives, that propelled him toward a deep course of reading and thinking about the stock market. Al was at work in 1969 on his Ph.D. thesis, "The Concept of Consciousness in Higher Education," when a young stockbroker in

Los Angeles suggested Al buy 30 shares of a company called Whittaker, which was then selling at $25 per share.
The stock bottomed at 1⅛, and Al got badly burned.

In irritation, Al began to read everything he could about stock market analysis, eventually coming upon the classic *The Intelligent Investor* by Ben Graham. Graham's theories about spotting cheap stocks made sense, and Frank joined the encampment of "value" investors, though speculation was always what he thought the process of investing really was. Frank still analyzes stocks in search of those issues whose potential market values are twice their going price. He hunts down stocks with growth rates around twice the normal rate, and he looks at a company's cash flow against its growth, its price against cash flow. In search of ratios, he places against one another some 30 numbers that are either publicly available or calculable from public sources. He preaches patience, diversification, and a careful selection process that has surfaced 600 stocks over the years. Around 25 percent have failed to thrive. He rarely sells out positions, and he never visits companies, because "everything I need to know is public."

Unlike many of his newsletter-writer peers, Al Frank does not tend to advertise, nor does he spend a lot of time on the road at investment conferences in search of subscribers. "I know I should," he said. "But I find that too often this business is very . . . well . . . sleazy."

Though outlandish and doctored performance claims are an aspect of the newsletter trade, a certain amount of control has been offered to consumers by another newsletter, one that does not pick stocks. Over the past 12½ years *The Hulbert Financial Digest* has tracked the performance of some of the most popular letters and has offered analysis of the newsletter market. In 1983, 28-year-old Mark Hulbert started tracking the performance record of *The Prudent Speculator*, which at the time circulated to only 75 individuals. Frank's 72.9 percent gain for 1983 was the best of all the letters Hulbert tracked, and in 1985 Hulbert reported that Frank's 272.9 percent five-year performance was also number one in the industry.

Mark Hulbert's discovery of Al Frank ("If I'm Dinah Shore, he's my Eddie Cantor," Frank mused one afternoon) led to thousands of new subscriptions for Frank and numerous appearances on television. By the middle of 1987, Al was grossing $1 million from subscriptions alone and another $1 million from managing other people's money according to his value-hunting principles. But "hoarded wealth invites attack," as Al once wrote in a letter, quoting Lao Tzu, "and wealth that is heavily leveraged is the most vulnerable of all."

The speculative component of Frank's prudent speculation includes a heavy penchant for buying stocks on margin. During 1986 his portfolio actually appreciated by only 16.9 percent. The Dow beat him with 27.4 percent that year (though he had beaten the Dow eight of nine years at that point). But because Al Frank borrows money from his brokerage house to purchase up to twice the number of stocks when he makes a buy, his 1986 portfolio actually returned 76.36 percent on equity. The hypothetical cash value of Frank's own portfolio since 1977 is up 411 percent (against the Dow's 245 percent), but his actual margined portfolio is up 742 percent, this because of the leverage that weighs in, every dollar of appreciation representing $2.

Al says that he got into margining when he realized that his original $8,000 could buy $16,000 worth of stocks and thus comprise a much more diversified portfolio. For a long time, Al Frank prospered in double-time. But the problem with trading on margin is the way a price drop comes back at you like a whirling boomerang. As profits are magnified by margin positions, losses double up too. If a stock goes below a point where 25 percent—or sometimes 30 percent—of its value is equity, a margin call from the brokerage house ensues, and you have to pony up in cash or sell out.

Al Frank got margin calls in spades during October 1987. He had to sell out some of his favorite stocks, and after the dust settled, he had parted with more than 55 percent of his portfolio. Few superstars were harder hit by the crash. Subscription cancellations soon outnumbered new subscriptions. Al employed 15 people before;

soon it was just the research director and Vicki Baldwin, Al's editor and wife.

By 1989, aided once again by the enhancements of margin, Al's portfolio was back up. He was one of only a handful of leading newsletter writers more than ten points above the S&P for the decade, and Mark Hulbert at one point rated him number one for the previous nine years of performance. But beneath the calm veneer, Al Frank's friends knew, he'd been set way back. He felt deeply for those who'd trusted his judgment and lost money during the crash because they sold—or were sold—out. "I couldn't believe the way people bailed out on Al," said fellow newsletter writer John Dessauer. "After all the money he'd made for people? He didn't lose his spirit, but he was badly hurt."

Over dinner in Santa Fe, Al seemed at peace remembering the crash. "The crash made me feel like my life was a movie. I took the big fall." Then he looked off into the corner of the Pink Adobe restaurant, reconsidering the interplay of life and money and a thousand other things.

"He just loves to think, too much," Vicki said later. "Al can't stop seeing all the dichotomies in things. He's always trying to figure everything out."

"In truth, he's boiling under the surface," said Al Frank's longtime friend, Los Angeles psychoanalyst Harvey Weintraub. "He worries. But he's knowledgeable and honest and I trust him with my money."

—

As we watched the market fall apart on TV that morning in Santa Fe—and when I heard Al Frank say "damn" and saw something less than peaceful in his light blue eyes and on his face—I knew I was seeing the crash again. "I should have bought some puts," I heard him say. "I hope it's not going to turn out to be like October of '87."

As for so many stockpickers of the buy-and-hold school—and as for so many other market professionals watching the 100-point free fall the day I was in Santa Fe—the Crash of 1987 turned Al Frank into something of a would-be market timer. *The Prudent Speculator* has for some time included paragraphs about OEX hedge strategies, about breakout patterns and the like. "If one is going to be heavily margined, then one must be a timer," Al explained, sounding resigned. Diversification—the protective tactic of choice for long-term investors—does not protect against a huge short-term sell-off, and Al Frank must avoid another short-term downswing because, though thousands of prospectuses claim otherwise, short-term performance is indeed the indication of future performance upon which most investors rely.

The big newsletter winner of 1987 was something called the *Puetz Investment Report.* Puetz was deeply into puts for all of 1987, down 86 percent before the crash, then up 500 percent and the winner for the year. Mark Hulbert has calculated that if you'd switched your investments into the recommendations of those newsletter writers who'd beaten the market in the previous year, at the end of each of the past ten years, you would have been up only 41 percent for the decade. But if you'd switched into those stocks recommended by those writers who hadn't beaten the market during the previous year, you would have been up 202 percent. Even five-year ratings are less than conclusive, though one academic study has shown that three-year records do begin to reveal elements of skill.

Another serious problem with tracking the past performance of any portfolio record—short-term or long, newsletter writer, money manager, or mutual fund—is that every newcomer to an investment association has to jump in at midstream. You could have bought all 20 stocks Al Frank recommended to subscribers at the end of December 1991 (they were up 29.2 percent as of November 1992, against 1.81 percent for the Dow), but you can't now assemble his model portfolio as he did without the use of a time machine.

So why should anyone depend on a newsletter?

Well, you shouldn't.

"You read a newsletter in order to develop a personal belief system that can be applied to the world," Al Frank says. "You read for the sheer liberation of gaining awareness about ourselves as *Homo eco-*

nomicus. Besides, newsletters contain better and less-compromised research than that offered by brokerage houses."

Investment newsletter readers are often written off as hobbyists, but inspired hobbyists are often superior students of their avocations. You read investment newsletters for entertainment and insight and for the challenge of following the thinking processes of people like Al Frank, who has dedicated many more waking hours than most people could possibly manage pondering the yin and yang of prices and markets. That Al Frank believes some wedding of inner peace and financial nirvana is possible for those who think hard enough about money and markets means that you and I don't have to take it quite that far. Al Frank's life's purpose has been to entwine "tranquility and profit," as he puts it. "We must know ourselves better than our stocks; we must deal with our own rationality more than with our stocks' ratios; we must cope with our transient irrationality more than with the fugitive fluctuations of our portfolios."

He thinks like this all the time, and somehow he manages to remain calmer than other men after being knocked cold.

As the market began to rebound from its 104-point trough the day I hung around Al Frank's Santa Fe office, he got up from his desk and announced it was time to go play tennis. And when the market finally closed that day after a rebound, with only a 22-point loss, Al was up in the mountains gazing at aspens. "They're golden now," he said before he left. "And . . . you can . . . see four . . . or five . . . states from the top."

The next morning, Al Frank, conquistador of the marketplace, was back at his cluttered desk, running numbers and plumbing the psychic deficiencies that form the intricate economy of the Golden Man that he could someday be.

Worth, February 1993

THE MASTER GRAPPLER

By the time I saw the huge snake cruising in, its black eyes rising just a quarter-inch above the primordial bog, I was submerged to my earlobes in a Louisiana bayou so completely decorated by plant and insect life and so thickly muddied by alluvial silt that the master catfish grappler beside me looked for all the world as if he'd been buried alive. We were two disembodied faces, pointing up into a ghostly, ancient forest of desiccated cottonwoods heavily festooned with gauzy moss.

The dense curtains of moss sucked the noise of the day from the air, though the huge mosquitoes sitting atop the water beside me sounded like helicopters, and nearby bullfrogs the size of two-month-old kittens sounded like foghorns on ocean vessels.

And I could hear the big snake swimming my way. It sounded not unlike a rowboat oar being dragged through a still lake.

"Pat," I hissed. "Big snake."

But Pat Mire was concentrating. He kept disappearing under the surface of the cold and viscous Bayou Mallet. He was feeling around in the bed of the bayou, searching for holes big enough to house a 20- or 40- or 50-pound catfish, which he intended to catch with his bare hands.

"Pat, you got water moccasins down here, don't you?" I wondered, casually as I could.

"Yes sir," said Pat. Then he took another breath. When he came back up, several gigantic mosquitoes lighted on his high forehead and began to poke him with prongs that looked like safety pins.

At 39, Patrick Mire is considered both an accomplished student of Cajun folk culture and the best of all the grapplers—or *pêcheurs-le-main*, a term that translates as "hand fishers"—in the entire tri-parish region of Louisiana's Prairie Cajun country. Mires going back several generations have risen early in the morning, dressed up as if to go duck hunting, and proceeded, with their shoes and hats still on, into the local bayous, there to catch very big, uncommonly strong fish with their hands.

A grappler dives directly into the holes and huge hollow logs and stumps where the biggest catfish live. Once inside, he attempts to entice the heavily barbed animal, which looks and behaves like ten to 60 pounds of pure muscle packed into a slime-coated wetsuit, to swallow a bare hand. At the first tentative nibble, the grappler kind of pets the great grotesque head of the fish. Slowly at first, and then with whatever violence becomes necessary, he slides his other hand ever deeper into the fish's gullet, hoping to reach out through one pulsing gill slit and grab hold of the other hand.

The fish perceives this violation as you might perceive a strong man threading his hand into your mouth, through your sinuses and auditory canal, and out into the light through your ear. The violent underwater confrontation that ensues often results in a 225-pound tough guy being dragged underwater and down toward the Gulf of Mexico by an animal with a pedigree dating back to the dinosaurs. On a good day—depending on the hand fisher involved—the man wins.

"You got to grab 'em there," Pat said when I asked if there wasn't a less disputed spot by which to lay hold of the fish. "They just too damned slick 'n' slimy and strong to grab anywhere else."

—

Most Cajun hand fishers will readily note that a catfish can "make you a bad sore," a reference to the fact that through a combination of particularly powerful jaw muscles and a mouth lined with high-grit sandpaper, a catfish can flay back the skin of a human arm and hand like so much peel off a ripe banana.

A typical catfish lying on the ground next to a river wears one of the meanest faces observable in all of nature. Given a few drops of water and a little mud, a catfish can kind of crawl off a bank and go home. (One exotic Asian breed is said to manage long portages through sheer willpower.) Catfish can bleat like wounded mammals at times, and if you stare hard enough, you can easily become convinced that an angry cat is just a half an evolutionary step from rising up, kicking your ass, and eating you whole.

The Catfish Book, a wonderful volume by Linda Crawford, reports Russian catfish measuring 15 feet in length and weighing in at 750 pounds. Mark Twain once reported the sighting of a 250-pound specimen on the Mississippi, and the fish can still get up around 200 pounds. Catfish apocrypha are of an appropriate scale: Waterfowl, various pets, and one small child—the poor youngster placed in stories all over history and locale—have all been snapped up by hungry cats. Innumerable *pêcheurs-le-main* have been dragged to their deaths, locked up shoulder-deep in some big cat's jaws, though you won't find any names or dates.

"An Obsoloosa cat will just destroy a hand," Pat had said when we stopped in at Mowata Store, his friend Bubba Frey's country eating place, for supplies (ice and lots of beer) before wading into Bayou Mallet. Mowata Store lies eight miles outside Eunice, Louisiana, right in the middle of Cajun country.

"A flathead is easier to handle," Pat continued. "Grab his lip just right and get his jaw outa position, and you're okay."

"You really goin' in?" Bubba asked me, just enough disbelief in his voice to make me nervous.

I'd agreed to be the guy who blocks the fish's escape route. I had no intention of feeling the inside of a catfish's mouth. There are few things better to eat than a well-cooked catfish, but the truth is I've always found the live version of the meal too repugnant of aspect even to touch.

Bubba pulled out from a great steel pot a couple of his hand-packed boudin sausages, delicious Cajun creations just hot enough to singe your nose hair. Bubba is known far and wide for his boudin and for his capacity to play an extremely clean Cajun fiddle, but his loyalty to the proud traditions of his culture stops just short of grapplin' with the cats in the bayou. "They'll roll you on over and take you down," he said, tugging at his T-shirt.

Bubba showed me a significant scar on his thumb where one of the local loggerhead snapping turtles once removed a bit of flesh. Loggerheads, Pat had explained, favor the same kind of holes catfish do.

"Loggerhead's got a head on him big as a 12-inch softball," Bubba said. "Things can take half your foot away."

He grinned at me. "So you really goin' in?" he asked again. I just smiled and shot a trusting look at Pat.

—

Out at the bayou, Pat and I donned suitable protective hand-fishing gear—jeans, sneakers, and long-sleeved flannel shirts. Pat loitered quite a while alongside his pickup, heartily diminishing a case of beer and talking of catfish battles past. He sorted out piles of red and purple mesh crawfish sacks that would be used both to stop up escape holes and bring the fish to shore. He wound a rope around his waist to hold the sacks, just as his father had taught him to do when Pat was only six.

Felix Mire, a farmer and retired butane delivery man, still joins Pat in the mud at 70. He likes to string a rope through the fish's mouth and out the gill slit when he grapples it, which makes it easier to drag the catch up onto the bank.

"You really comin' in?" Pat said, his tone causing me to think upon the preimmersion beer as part sacramental Cajun tradition and part application of a liquid foolhardiness sufficient to the craziness at hand.

Then we got wet.

Walking in a slow-moving bayou is a special sensation. You'd move slowly even if you hadn't heard it was safer that way, because each step deposits you thigh-deep in fine delta silt. This water was icy, and the air didn't move at all.

Up along the tributarial edges of the Kankakee River in Illinois, where I first heard about men catching the least sightly of all freshwater fish with their bare hands, the little-known pastime is called "hogg'n'." In Arkansas, where it's against the law, they call it "noodlin'." In East Texas, it's called "grabblin'," while in certain parts of Louisiana it's called "grapplin' " or "grabbin'." In Mississippi, where the emphasis falls more to the tactile mesmerization of the fish than to the actual wrestling of the animal onto the land, they call it "charming." "Graveling" and "hand grabbing" are other variations on the same sport—if sport is what this tribal bit of manly endeavor can accurately be called.

Technique and style vary according to region and relative claim to historical tradition—the most outlandish variation I've come across being the application of a protective layer of duct tape to the hand and forearm. All practitioners share a reverent tone when they claim to understand certain transcendent secrets tethered to the dying art. I often heard that a grandfather or a great-grandfather had learned how to do it, usually from somebody who lived downriver, farther to the south. I kept asking who invented hand fishing—who was the first to even imagine such a thing—and I asked all the way down to the bayous of south-central Louisiana until I found a window to a deeper past. In Pat Mire's isolated piece of the republic, Cajun men say they learned to put their hands into a big fish's mouth from the local Indians, and the local Indians claim they've just known how to do it all along.

A few years ago, Pat Mire made a film about hand fishing in the bayous called *Anything I Catch: The Handfishing Story.* In it, he reported that an old-timer was once asked what he did when a snake occupied the hole he was exploring instead of a fish.

"Why, you jus' find yo' another hole," the old-timer said.

I kept thinking about the line as the big snake swam closer. I was sure I saw it smiling. I kept looking over at Pat, just to make sure he saw it too. I sensed that an intricate etiquette was involved in joining the animals in the swamp. I tried to stay cool like Pat.

"Whoa, Pat," I said. "Before you go back down, just tell me if this big snake here is poisonous."

I watched four huge mosquito bites enlarge on Pat's head like small balloons. He seemed oblivious now, as if he'd moved into some altered, meditative state. He was actually "fishing," feeling things with his feet, occasionally touching submerged logs with his hands and then diving down to feel the edges of holes in the banks. He'd said the catfish—*goujon,* as the Cajuns call them—tend to smooth out the entrances to their holes.

"Don't worry," he said. "I can smell water moccasins. You know, my dad, he won't ever back away from a snake. He feels one in a hole, and he grabs it by the tail and tosses it up on the bank. I've seen him throw water moccasins out many a time.

"Now, come on under and feel this log," he said. I jumped when he grabbed my hand under the clouded water. He directed me to a huge log, the hole in its side marked by rough and deep ax cuts.

"Very old," Pat said. "Even in the late 19th century they would have used a rough-cut saw. Not many people have ever felt this log. They put the hole there to block off one side of the log. Okay, now. Let's just see if we got a fish inside."

I bunched up some crawfish sacks as Pat instructed and plunged my hands into the hole. I could barely keep my mouth above the surface, and I was sure that much of one hand was still exposed to whatever lurked inside the log.

"If you feel a bump, don't move," Pat said as he felt his way to the far side of the log, moving in huge, elliptical steps, like an astronaut across a stretch of moon. "The hardest thing to learn is not to move when he touches you. Just try. If you jerk back from a loggerhead, that's when he clamps off whatever he's got in his mouth."

"Can they see us, Pat?"

"Who?"

"The fish."

"Who knows?" he said, drawing in a big breath.

And with that, Pat went under, and in the next second I felt a powerful, wriggling force slam like a hard-swung baseball bat against my bare hand.

—

The Cajuns are descended from the French Acadians, whom the British deported from Nova Scotia in 1755. They began fishing with their hands because the nets and weirs their fishermen brought south didn't work in the tideless swamps and bayous of Louisiana. Over the years, as the refugees and their descendants and additions settled in the boggiest realms of the Deep South, they were known first as Cadiens and finally as Cajuns, the term applied by locals with whom they blended through the years. " 'Cajun'—as 'Indian' became 'Injun,' " Pat explained.

Most of Pat's films are based on his research into Cajun folkways. He left Eunice after college and grew out his hair. He hit the gringo trail in South America and lived on the Kenai Peninsula in Alaska.

"I came back starving for this," Pat said as we floated and shivered in the morass. "I came back for the music, the food, the talk, and to do things like this—things that set us apart from other people."

The previous evening, out at Bubba's uncle's camp, some men had gathered for Cajun music and Cajun food and, apparently, to compare their scars. A local rice farmer was contending that it was a "big ol' blue cat" that had years ago pulled the skin off his left thumb.

"That's not what you said last time," somebody replied.

Camps are a Cajun institution. The one owned by Bubba's uncle is a ramshackle two-room dwelling with a big table and a bunch of plastic kitchen chairs. The 13,000 inhabitants of Eunice have seen better times than now, with the oil business dried up. The camps become more important when it gets like this.

Though the camp is not far from town, the area nearby is heavily wooded. Hooks and chains for skinning fish and game protruded from several trees. An extremely heavy iron pot, very black, was sitting on a fire. Pat whipped up a fragrant catfish étouffée; a tray full of fat catfish steaks and another full of bullfrog legs the size of jackrabbit hinds sat nearby. Cayenne pepper was poured into the pot, and strangely sad and medieval music filled the night.

Pat was stirring in time with the music when somebody said, "We shoulda invited some women."

"What, and fuck the whole thing up?" Bubba replied.

I told Pat that a senior parks-and-wildlife official in Texas had told me that Texas, like Arkansas, outlawed grapplin' because it was thought unsporting, tantamount to dynamiting or electrifying a body of water. The official had added that catfish that will let you get a hand in their mouths are usually spawning. "One of those boys gets real good at it," the man had said, "and he can clean out a river."

"First," Pat said, "it's the male that guards the hole. The male shoves the female in there, but then she leaves. He stands guard until the eggs are hatched, upon which he begins to eat as many of his children as he can. I pull out a big old male, and the babies live. As to it not being sporting—compared to the sporting way of tricking a fish into thinking there's no steel hook inside his food—I jus' don't know what to say."

Several of the men at the camp offered me ironic compliments about my plan to follow Pat into a swamp full of snakes, turtles, and a particularly trashy sort of fish that's changed little since the Eocene epoch. One or two put their one arm not holding a beer around me and said that I must be fully accoutred in the anatomical sense.

By the time his transcendent étouffée was ladled over plates of steaming rice, Pat was sitting on one of the frayed plastic chairs, waving away mosquitoes and trying to explain what you have to know to risk the primal vagaries of deep, dark holes. He tried to talk of what you had to feel inside to be able to convince a great big fish to fall into your grasp.

"You have to become part of the environment; you have to feel part of the same exact thing as that fish. You have to become larger than your own impulses. And you have to really use those hands."

As he spoke, I thought about watching my six-year-old daughter playing in a pond a few weeks earlier. Several of her friends had been trying time and again to capture one of the hundreds of darting newts that teemed below the pond's surface. As the others gave up in frustration, my daughter—who likes to stand back and take in a scene before plunging in—slowly put one hand into the pond and waited. She drew it out and handed a wriggling newt to one of her friends. Then she reached back in and came out with another, handing a newt to each of her playmates, steady and calm. I waded in and tried to catch one for ten minutes, obviously out of sync, utterly in awe.

"I do it because it won't be done much longer," Pat was saying by the time the fiddles were being packed away. "I fish with my hands, well, jus' 'cause I can."

———

"Be mentally prepared," Pat said before he went down after the fish again. "Concentrate on not drawing back."

By now my feet had floated to the surface, but I was determined to block up the hole. A hogger from up north had told me that in the eight-foot waters he fished, one man will stand on a submerged hogger's back and others will pile on until sufficient weight is brought to bear to keep the bottom guy down; other times, two men will dive down and physically insert another into a deep hole.

Pat was underwater for a very long time. He had told me that in the old days a hand fisher who could spend a few minutes underwater was revered as a true *plonger.* Pat said it often takes some time to stroke and pet the fish.

"Otherwise they get wild," he said. (All the talkers on the subject pronounce it "while.") "And a wild cat you really don't need. You have to slowly feel what you've got. Then you've got to move in."

I felt another hard bump. Whatever hit me was very hard and even colder than the frigid water. Seconds later Pat shot out of the bayou, rising up like a Polaris missile, gasping for air. His left hand was spurting blood from having been deeply spined, but he was hugging a hideous-looking bit of prehistory to his chest, clutching as the fish slapped him hard in the gut.

When the fish was finally glowering in the dust beside the bayou, two bare-chested teenagers in feed-store caps strolled onto the bank. "You the boy made the fee-ulm," one of them said to Pat.

"You teach us to fish?" said the other. "My great-grandfather could do it, but I don't know anybody who still knows how."

"Yeah, sure," Pat said, panting, bleeding, his wound swelling up like an extra digit, insect bites rising from his pate, mud coating his soaked clothes. "I'll teach you."

The two boys smiled broadly as the incensed catfish below them just stared off into the eerie woods.

Outside, October 1992

GOOD TIMES COMIN' IN ARKANSAS

One time there was a feller from Illinois, and he heard a lot of wild tales about Arkansas. . . ."

More than one of the old stories begins like that.

I first heard about Arkansas when I was a small boy in Chicago. My great-uncle, Dave Katz, used to sit on the edge of one of our comfortable chairs during his trips north and talk about the fish and rivers and woods of his Ozarks. I knew he was considered a real pioneer in Harrison, Arkansas, and I wondered how a real American pioneer could be from Germany and say "dat one" and "ja." I remember that he could predict the weather from the hue of a passing cloud and gauge a tree's ripeness for cutting by the way it rang. His association with the old things in the woods caused him to be known to the country around Harrison as Uncle Dave, and when he died (I was 12), we were told that "the boys" from the U.S. Forest Service had scattered Dave's ashes near his favorite Ozark hill.

Out of the old Sunday afternoon conversations, the ancient hills of the Arkansas Ozarks became a special place for me because, somehow, Uncle Dave always seemed like the brave men in books.

On my mother's side of the family were our Arkansas flat-landers. Louis Altheimer, my great-great-grandfather, sailed from Germany in 1863 at the age of 14, convinced that the truly "brave and free" men of his time lived in Arkansas. He had discovered this in a popular book by a German named Friedrich Gerstaecker, who wrote glowingly of horse thieves and duels in Arkansas. (Other writers of the time dwelled on the early Arkansans' penchant for "gougin'" eyeballs and "castratin'.") Arkansas was the ambivalent edge of human civilization then, the meeting place of barbarian and pioneer. It had been explored by Spaniards almost a century before the Pilgrims arrived at Plymouth Rock, named by Frenchmen, taken from Indians, worked by the descendants of Africans, and owned by a "lordly race" of Anglo-Saxon planters. It was just the spot for a German Jewish boy fleeing from one of the most settled existences that history had yet offered, back on the banks of the Rhine.

Louis rode the range in Wyoming with Buffalo Bill Cody for a while. Then he came back to Pine Bluff, a backwater area even by Arkansas standards. He cleared and drained alluvial swampland for a large plantation and convinced the Cotton Belt Railroad to run tracks by his farm. A depot was built, and Louis Altheimer had himself a town: Altheimer, Arkansas. He had conquered a chunk of the New World called by nothing less than his own family name. As he noted in an autobiographical essay modestly titled "Louis Altheimer, Empire Builder," Arkansas had been kind.

Louis' Arkansas was that of the halcyon days of the past century. His son Maurice labored through Arkansas's dark days with the family plantation, and Maurice's son, Alan Altheimer—my grandfather—told me Arkansas tales 45 years after leaving the place.

"When I was six years old," he said, "the bigger boys at school came and put us in the deep window wells that surrounded the school. They called the window wells Jew pits, and the teachers had to come get us out. I proceeded to fight my way through school until I got to high school. I saw a hundred thousand Ku Klux Klansmen march down Main Street in Little Rock—a hundred thousand of them. I saw crosses burning, and there were lynchings during my childhood. I saw the boll weevils eat the crops and the floods wash them away, and I saw drought dry them up. . . ."

Then he went to college in New York City. During a visit home in 1920, he accompanied his father on a trip to the family farm, 50 miles southeast of Little Rock. On Main Street in Altheimer, he was introduced to a black man, so he extended his hand. "Alan," his father said afterward, "don't ever do that again. You don't shake a black man's hand in Altheimer. If anybody'd seen you, I'd never be able to come back here."

"Poppa," my grandfather said, "I'm not coming back to Arkansas."

And he didn't. He moved to Chicago after graduating from law school and returned to Arkansas only for visits and funerals, the last time for the funeral of the last white Arkansas Altheimer in 1948.

———

Thousands of people fled Arkansas as my grandfather did, faster and faster with each successive decade, blacks going to Chicago or Detroit, whites opting for California. There were fewer people in Arkansas in the 1960s than before World War II—hardly the national trend.

Bad things just seemed to rain on the state of Arkansas, and good things blew on by like the topsoil. After the Civil War, in which most Arkansans fought for the South, bones protruded from the earth during rainstorms for many years. Disproportionate numbers of young Arkansas men went off to America's 20th-century wars, and a disproportionate number never returned. In 1927, the Mississippi River and its tributaries inundated one fifth of the entire state in what Herbert Hoover called "the greatest peacetime disaster in our history." In 1930, the worst drought on record gripped the South and Southwest, including Arkansas. The following year, one third of the state's residents faced starvation.

Arkansans appeared the only defeated Americans of the nation's second century. The thirties in Arkansas lasted well into the fifties, right up until an army of the North occupied the capital of the state in 1957. Somebody's sneering mother appeared on television sets around the world carrying a rowboat oar toward the steps of Little Rock Central High School. In minutes, she transformed an image of grinding poverty and infant mortality into a picture of racism of such virulence that the state, the city of Little Rock, and a governor named Orval Faubus were emblazoned on the consciousness of the time as universal symbols of American wickedness.

After Little Rock, Arkansas lay locked in cultural, economic, and spiritual stasis for a decade. Its original pioneer dream of spirit, landscape, gristle, and gut lay inert. When news bellowed forth of the hatred and the massive resistance to change that had been characteristic of the state of Arkansas for all of his long life, my grandfather—along with the former Arkansans at the aircraft plants in California and in the tenements of the northern ghettos—simply assumed that was exactly what the people of Arkansas wanted.

Thus, 22 years after Little Rock, I still understood his reaction when I told him I proposed to visit Arkansas.

"Arkansas!" he said as my grandmother gasped in the background. "You're going to Arkansas?"

"It's changed," I said. "The grandchildren of your generation are returning now, and the young people aren't leaving anymore." I told him about the hippies and the back-to-the-land types and the retirees in the Ozark hills. I talked about the infusion of new ideas, the prosperity that was beginning to overtake the poverty, the progressivism that had always been there emerging from behind the reaction. I mentioned the new governor, 33, and the secretary of state and attorney general, then both 32—three leaders who, according to one writer, "have yet to require the assistance of the second track of their Trac II razors."

I said I was going to roam the forgotten state, meet the people who were directing its renaissance, and even go back to Altheimer, Arkansas, to the old family plantation for which my great-great-grandfather once publicly thanked his good star.

"Well, I'll be damned," my grandfather said. "Back to Arkansas."

—

So armed with memories of the old stories, a new road map, and an appointment with the governor, I lit out for the new Arkansas, unlikely mecca for a new decade and most recent repository of the hope for the American millennium.

The state has never quite decided in which part of the country it feels most comfortable. It's the meeting place of North, South, and West, straddling the geographies of southern plantation land, isolated midwestern highlands, and flat, rangy western prairie. The different forces on every side produce a sectionalism within the state that is more like that of England than of most parts of the United States. Terrain, history, political attitudes, traditions, and especially accents change with every geographical move.

In the northwest corner of Arkansas, Highway 74 spirals east into the delicate, almost frail hills of Madison County. It continues deep into the interior, abruptly shifting from gravel to gray dirt and then back to powdery blacktop, through a corridor of rural counties that are among the most gorgeous, least populated, and poorest in the nation. The houses, many far from the uneven two-rut tracks that pass for roads in the Ozarks, are built in the vernacular architecture of poor people. Over a third of them have no running water.

These ancient hills were the preserve of mountaineers whose ancestors stopped there because it reminded them of Ireland or England. If you eavesdrop on conversations or monitor the CB radio, you can still hear Ozarkers saying "hain't" and "twixt" and "yon side" as people did in 16th-century England. But only the adults speak that way now. Most of their children talk like the people on television.

For a long time, the hill people were staples of American comedy—caricatures who could be depended on to retain their quirks. Li'l Abner, Mammy Yokum, and Daisy Mae came from Arkansas. The northern part of the state was said to be peopled by unaltered rustics, heavily muscled, barefoot illiterates. They supposedly ignored not only progress but also liquor laws, criminal laws, political change, taxes, and even the incest taboo.

Granny Friar never cared about the cartoon caricatures. She named one daughter Cummie May and has 24 grandchildren with similar names. Granny wears dilapidated gym shoes and carries a .45 pistol under her skirt. Her tiny face is imploded like an apple doll's, and the area in front of her little house is littered with old refrigerators, engine blocks, and a vivid history of washing machines that extends back to the rusty pail.

Granny Friar lives among a few sunburnt hilltops in Madison County in a place appropriately called Friartown. She named it. There is no sign because "ever'body knows where 'tis." The dogs start to howl when Granny talks to strangers, as if it's a noise they aren't used to.

"On 'bout ten years ago, I could pull logs on over that hill, but now best ah kin do is go down ta feed the hogs," she told me. Granny said that it's important to keep active; she was critical of one of her sons, who used to raise fighting cocks, because "he's so old 'n' decrepit, all he does is jus' set. Haw! Jus' set. . . . It's a damn good life up here. Ya work when ya want ta. Set when ya want ta."

I asked if she'd seen changes in the hills.

"Ah bin here all my life an' ain't seen nothin' yet," she said above the canine howls. "Jus' me, the dogs 'n' the hogs—'n' course there's the hippies in the holler."

The hippies in the hollow are some of the many Americans, representing a farrago of life-styles and philosophies, who have suddenly immigrated into a region that remained isolated and poor for a long time. In the first seven years of the 1970s, some Ozark counties doubled in population—and the population of the state as a whole grew 11.5 percent. The biggest increase was among the 20-to-24-year-old group, a combination of newcomers and upwardly mobile Ozark natives who are staying put for the first time this century.

Old and new mix gingerly but without much hostility. In the town of Kingston, in the eastern part of Madison County, only a few buildings surround an empty square, but each is covered with its own lovely pattern of hammered tin. One building is a café, and in the middle of the café is a huge glass beehive teeming with fat, crusty bees. The pulsing labyrinth is connected to the outside by a clear glass tube that is badly stained. Arrowhead collections are framed on the walls, and there's a bumper-pool table, but most of the customers appear to watch the bees.

The waitress stopped to talk with me about Madison County. She said they had dances sometimes in Kingston.

Then she leaned forward. "And we got lizzes," she said.

"Oh, lizards," I said.

The waitress blushed. "Naow. Ah mean—*lezz*es."

"Oh. Lesbians?"

She gasped but nodded.

There is indeed a small lesbian commune in Madison County, I learned later, and there are larger populations of young gays in nearby areas. One northern Arkansas town has a thriving gay-dominated night life. Back in Fayetteville, the home of the famous University of Arkansas football team, the Razorbacks, there is an organization of gay women called the Razordykes.

—

The back-to-the-landers, some hippies and some not, are another kind of newcomer to the Ozarks. As I traveled through Carroll, Madison, Newton, and the other rural counties where my uncle Dave Katz once hunted white oak for his barrels, I could tell which valleys were occupied by new people by the presence of small Japanese tractors in the yards. The natives buy American.

In one of the most desolate back reaches of the Ozarks, I found two of the more successful Arkansas immigrants. Above the tiny town of Parthenon, rimmed by high cliffs bearing white columnlike formations, Dan and Mary Lou Taylor live on 160 acres. They won a $10,000 award in the Food Self-Sufficiency Competition held by the *Mother Earth News* in 1977. "I searched from the Panama Canal to the Arctic Circle for an unindustrialized spot, the right spot," Dan said.

He and Mary Lou, aided by the knowledge he acquired getting a doctorate in chemical engineering, have devised a life for themselves that involves only minuscule input from the outside and very little need for any money at all. Their farm is full of brilliant, beautiful contraptions that use water and muscle power to generate all of the Taylors' electricity and process their food.

But the award inspired a report about their lives on the CBS news one night, and the Taylors came to be treated "like shrines." "We only became children of the times, as far as I'm concerned, when the TV cameras arrived," Dan said. "Want to hear my list of complaints about the outside assumptions about us? First, we are not into nostalgia for the old times. We do not have 'free' food just because we don't use money. My invested man-hours to produce a loaf of bread far exceed those of someone buying it in a store. We are not 'big pinchers'—people who think we'll be in great shape when the crunch comes. We are not missionaries, examples to others. And we are not out of the rat race. The rat race of my existence here is far more harrowing than outside. There's nothing more to all this than that this is where Mary Lou and I want to be."

The gays, communards, serious back-to-the-land farmers, artists, craftsmen, Ph.D.'s running stores, the random representatives of the alternative youth international of the times who hang out in Arkansas, are all loosely referred to as the "new culture." At a "lyin'" contest in the preserved 19th-century town of Eureka Springs, native Ozarkers sat straight-backed in their windbreakers and overalls along with many new culture families. The scene looked as if someone with a marking pen had defaced Norman Rockwell's *Freedom of Speech* by adding various moustaches and beards. The winning lie was told by the Eureka Springs police chief, a young Robert Redford look-alike who'd been a Californian only four months earlier. "It was so damn hot this summer," he had drawled like a native in his winning effort, "that I saw two trees chasin' a dog."

"The new folks don't really fit in, but you know, that's okay, too," one Madison County official said. "Oh, ever' once in a while some of 'em grow a little too mucha that marijuana an' the sheriff has to go back an' harvest it fer 'em, but hell—you know? I mean, hell."

———

There are other new Arkansans in the Ozarks whose presence is no less conspicuous or incongruous than that of the most countercultural Madison County lizards. The roads up at the Missouri border are cluttered with large signs announcing the entrances to instantaneous walled villages whose names end with words like Acres, Hills, Estates, and City. These are little insulated islands of white middle-class affluence nestled in relatively untouched rural beauty, each complete with its own police department, medical clinic, restaurants—and no Arkansans. The appeal to the elderly retirees from Illinois or Pennsylvania who account for half of the Ozark population boom is, according to one Eureka Springs resident, "fresh air, clean water, low taxes, and no crime"—"crime" being a delicate euphemism for which several retirees were quite ready to substitute "Negroes." Even though a short drive takes you into cotton counties that are as heavily populated by blacks as any in the country, the Ozarks somehow remain devoid of blacks.

The retirees and the back-to-the-landers are only the latest in a long stream of pioneers, false messiahs, and dreamers who have marched to their private cadence in the direction of the Ozarks. And while the natives shun mundane visitors such as government bureaucrats, they have treated the influx of those of an individual mind with tolerance—in fact, they sort of like it. There is a viable camaraderie of poverty that exists between the back-to-the-lander and the unreconstructed native, despite backgrounds as different as any two groups in the country could have. The hillbillies and longhairs share a strong respect for human individuality, a bullheaded sense of environmental protectionism, a mild lawlessness, a basic communitarianism, and a low opinion of the relative value and healthiness of industrialized society. It is as if the old-timers stayed poor all this time because they were waiting for a generation to come along that would see things their way and help to preserve their values.

The Ozarks are among the six cleanest areas in the nation environmentally; the nearest of the hundreds of U.S. cities that the Environmental Protection Agency considers polluted is 125 miles away. But with the influx of people and money, Ozark residents are scrambling to preserve those parts of tradition and landscape that are too delicate to withstand overdevelopment. There is much talk of appropriate technology and the sustenance of the Ozark "bioregion."

Still, the most striking thing about Arkansas today is its infinite variety. Hidden away in the 53,000 unruined square miles of the state in significant numbers are not only environmentalists but also developers, preindustrial hillbillies, postindustrial members of the new culture, aristocratic deep-Delta planters, former sharecroppers, Proposition 13–style retirees, and people who believe government still can and should remedy injustice.

———

There is also in Arkansas a burgeoning new political elite that the invigorated populace has elected to lead it into the light. The current leader in the state is Governor Bill Clinton, 33. When a regional junior college presidents' association assembled recently in the rickety spa city of Hot Springs, its chairman delivered an introduction of the governor that would have gotten them both run out of Arkansas 15 years ago: ". . . a Rhodes scholar, Yale Law graduate, a law professor, brilliant, brilliant wife, about to have a brilliant baby, handsome, the youngest attorney general in America, the nation's youngest governor, the youngest governor of Arkansas in 134 years, bound for national politics . . ." The man stopped after a while and looked at the kid sitting next to him. "May I ask you a question?" he said. "What the hell do you worry about?"

Bill Clinton turned down an offer to work on the Watergate Committee staff in 1974 in order to come home and run for Congress at the age of 27. He lost, but Arkansans liked him. He won the job of attorney general in 1976 and then won many more friends by taking on the hated utility companies.

Warnings by Frank Lady, Clinton's opponent for the governorship in 1978, that Clinton was the most liberal man ever to seek office in Arkansas had no effect on the results of the election. Clinton did run George McGovern's campaign in Texas in 1972, and he had worked on Project Pursestrings, the student lobby to cut off funding for the Vietnam War. But he would have gone to Vietnam if he was drafted—which he almost was.

Today, Clinton presides over a state administration that reminded me of a college yearbook staff; in each office, the governor's (Clinton, 33), the attorney general's (Steve Clark, now 33) and the secretary of state's (Paul Riviere, 32), the youngest face belongs to the boss. When I asked one young Clinton aide how "hip" a governor's office can get and still be taken seriously, she said, "Well, we all still shave our legs."

But Clinton really isn't a fiery young progressive who has changed Arkansas by force of character or ideology. He is more a culmination of the renaissance of spirit in Arkansas and the logical conclusion of the radical changes in the state over the past 12 years working in concert with the finer strain of a long and often noble political tradition. "I'm more a reflection than one who's created," he said at breakfast one morning. "I'm comfortable within the stream of Arkansas history."

Arkansas history had flowed only a few weeks earlier at the funeral of former attorney general Bruce Bennett, a jowly, silver-haired race-baiter who was once indicted on 27 counts of fraud but who managed to get the trial delayed so long on grounds of ill health that the matter was eventually forgotten altogether. At Bennett's obsequies, "Justice" Jim Johnson showed up along with old Marlin Hawkins, the infamous sheriff and political kingpin of Conway County. Hawkins is famous for many things in Arkansas, not the least of which is his wandering glass eye, which he claims to take out at night and set up on the windowsill of his bedroom "ta keep a' eye on things in my county" while he is asleep. "You jus' gonna write what a mean ole man ah am, jus' like the other Yankee reporters come down here below the Smith 'n' Wesson Line," Marlin said on the phone when I asked for an interview after Bruce Bennett's funeral. "Smith 'n' Wesson Line"—that's what he said.

Marlin's companion, Jim Johnson, never ran a county machine like Hawkins. Jim's thing was caustic racist invective. A certain Arkansan respect for first-rate Bible-thumpin' homiletics—however hateful and mad they may be—kept Johnson running seriously for high public office in Arkansas until 1976. Johnson is Arkansas's leading example of a hard-seg, clear-throated, back-slappin', Bible-beatin', red-blooded, all-American, down-home southern demagogue. Jim's trademarks are a homburg and a striped tie, one deaf ear, refusing to shake hands with blacks, prejudicial terms of endearment for everyone he's ever known, and an ugly organization called the White Citizens Council, which brought Jim considerable exposure in 1957.

Orval Faubus himself once described Justice Jim as a "purveyor of hate." Faubus later claimed it was Jim's racist proddings that caused him to cross the line he drew in the dust back in 1957, during what Arkansans still call "the crisis." Faubus, who manipulated the state for 12 years, was such a creature of the politics of human fear that many people still believe he wasn't a real racist. He was hung in effigy in foreign countries after paratroopers occupied Little Rock so nine black children could go to school, but in Arkansas, he won his next election by a larger margin than ever. Up in Granny Friar's Madison County, where Orval was born, they turned out over 100 percent of the vote for their boy. They worshipped him.

Though few people outside Arkansas are aware of it, when Orval Faubus first emerged out of those hills, he was fundamentally a liberal, humane individual. His background was actually well to the left of liberalism. His father, Sam Faubus, was an active socialist, a devotee of Eugene Victor Debs—which is less surprising than it sounds. Arkansas's sullied image of intolerance in more recent years has obscured the state's historical role as the nursery of American agrarian radicalism and various other forms of unsophisticated egalitarianism. In the first two decades of this century, independent, conservative Arkansas had nine thriving socialist newspapers. When Huey P. Long was seven years old, Arkansas already had a governor who had come to power by running against the railroads, invoking antitrust laws as attorney general, and representing the "plain people of our country." He was later labeled "the Karl Marx for hillbillies."

As with so many other historical themes long since purged from other polities, the bundled tension of old-fashioned populism is still present in Arkansas, almost as if it had been pickled in brine. Throughout the days of Orval's many infamous antics as governor of Arkansas, a Madison County hill-dweller wrote letters, under a nom de plume, that violently criticized Faubus. Only after old Sam's death was it revealed that Orval's critic had been his own disapproving father.

———

In 1966, Orval finally retired and returned to the hills. He fell on hard times back in Madison County and ended up working at the local bank. His mantle passed to none other than Justice Jim Johnson, and amazingly, Jim was trounced in the elections by an Arkansas immigrant from New York City, a man whose family name indicated unconscionable private wealth to people who had never even heard of Orval Faubus or Arkansas.

Winthrop Rockefeller fled to Arkansas in search of solace and an inexpensive divorce in 1953. He found the solace atop a flat, high mesa—cleft by startling gorges and waterfalls—which he cleared and upon which he built a ranch. He became the first Republican governor of Arkansas since the end of Reconstruction, and by the time he died of cancer in 1973, it was clear that the color-blind immigrant, the Rockefeller who always feared he couldn't measure up to his brothers, had been the necessary prerevolutionary causeway between old and new, between Faubus and Bill Clinton.

Rockefeller gave government jobs to blacks and brought numerous non-defense-oriented industries into poverty-stricken towns. He also made it rather unfashionable to be a segregationist. Even the white business community began to see that there was money in tolerance. Blacks began to vote in increasing numbers. Then it turned out that Justice Jim hadn't paid his taxes, for all of his righteous raging, and in retrospect that Faubus had hypocritically abused the power born of Arkansas's love for him, and everyone sort of felt betrayed.

A handsome Sunday school teacher named Dale Bumpers emerged from nowhere and said quite simply that segregation was immoral. Bumpers appeared to have asked no one if he could run and owed no man a favor—and the electorate liked that. Bumpers hooked into the positive strains of the submerged populist spirit just as Orval had worked the negative ones, and in 1970, he ran successfully for governor against Faubus, who had come out of retirement for the occasion.

Thereafter, the new breed of Arkansas politicians made startling inroads:

In 1974, Senator J. William Fulbright, the stern, archetypal patrician intellectual, fell to Bumpers.

In 1977, Senator John McClellan died and was replaced by the Young Turk governor David Pryor, who first went to Congress from Arkansas at the age of 32.

In 1975, after being one of the hardest-working, most effective men in Washington, Congressman Wilbur Mills saw his career abruptly curtailed by his love for drink—an old story, newly revealed—and a topless dancer. He was replaced by a 33-year-old Harvard graduate named Jim Guy Tucker, who was previously Little Rock prosecuting attorney at 27 and Arkansas state attorney general at 29.

The transformation of Arkansas politics was not confined to the top of the political heap, moreover. The demand for rapid change combined with reemergence of the old populism to produce a new mood at the lowest levels of activity as well. The Arkansas Community Organizations for Reform Now (ACORN), currently the nation's most successful association of community activists, began operating under the Arkansas state motto—*Regnat populus* (The people rule). ACORN challenged corrupt local government, utility company abuses, and corporate power and tackled many other grass-roots issues. It attracted activists from all over the country into its weblike organization of largely poor Arkansas families—and then spread into 19 other states.

Organizations such as ACORN, the new leaders, the influx of such varied types of people, the fact that the state's youth was staying put, and a pervasive new vision of the future—all of these things—have pushed people like Justice Jim and Marlin Hawkins toward the edge of caricature. Nonetheless, Jim still speaks his mind in open public in Arkansas and is thinking of running again—maybe against Dale Bumpers for the Democratic senatorial nomination this year. At a time when other, much less vigorous southern states have long since sent their Justice Jims to the taxidermist, the old warhorses remain part of a stylistic tradition that Arkansans respect.

—

As I roamed the state last fall, signs of another combative Arkansas tradition appeared around every bend. On every movie theater marquee in every little town blessed with the movies, in front of every gas station, on every free billboard and pasted over some billboards that weren't free, on car bumpers, on T-shirts stretched over every topographical formation the human chest makes available—it was BEAT TEXAS! GO RAZORBACKS!

They came to the game in Hog-cars with protective Hog-flaps. The little snarling red razorback hog—an animal that never existed, though many Arkansas schoolchildren will tell you that "De Soto brought them or something"—adorned everything. And lording it over all others were those who wore the Hog Hat, one of the most fearsome inventions to come out of Arkansas since they stopped production at the biological warfare arsenal in Pine Bluff. In their thousands, Arkansans walked toward the stadium in the huge red plastic hats that depict a squatting razorback replete with tusks, six-inch snout, and an "A" branded on its sides. The angry, hideous animal squats there obscenely, enveloping the wearer's cranium all the way down to the smile. "SOOOOOOOOOOOO-eeeeEEEEE! PIG!" the fans roared to their Hogs, the Hogs down on the field.

Many rationalizations have been offered to explain Hogism, but most Arkansans are well aware of its true genesis—"It's just one of the first things in the world that this rundown ole state finally figured it could do well," a local newspaperman said. "That's all there is to it."

Arkansas has traditionally been near the top of the ladder in America only in white teenage pregnancy, the incidence of venereal disease—and college football. In a search for identity among two centuries' worth of symbols that include gouged eyeballs, the Depression, barefoot women, and a football team named after one of the less attractive creatures imaginable, the Hogs win hands down.

But even Hogism has been subtly transformed in the new Arkansas. As I scanned the crowd through a photographer's camera during the Razorback–University of Houston game and watched the faces contort in delight and pain, I came upon a particularly bright face beaming from a background of Hog Hats and realized it was Bill Clinton's. He was screaming, too.

Nowadays, many of the Arkansas football players wait for Clinton rather than a cheerleader to congratulate them outside the locker room. The notably intelligent quarterback of the Razorbacks, Kevin Scanlon, is already working in the governor's office and intends to pursue a career in Arkansas politics. So does 250-pound offensive tackle Phillip Moon. And many of the best students in the University of Arkansas law school intend to stay in the state and go into politics. "You see," Bill Clinton told me, "politics is still perceived as an honorable profession down here. And it is perceived as such by young men and women who want to be a part of it."

—

The remarkable fact is that while Arkansas is a comparatively poor and uneducated state, an unusually high percentage of its citizens turn out to vote, and polls show that its electorate is one of the best-informed in the nation about complex issues. Even more important, the polls show that Arkansans not only participate in politics, they still believe their participation makes a difference. "It's part of this faith in the possibility of progress, of doing better," Clinton said.

Clinton shares that faith. He has a specific idea of what Arkansas should be. Central to his vision is the idea that government—particularly state government—can still help people achieve their goals. This, of course, puts him at odds with the "enlightened" elite in a national political scene dominated by a sense of diminishing expectations.

All around Arkansas are states that have already made their big mistakes, but their talk of "belt tightening" has not spread to Arkansas. (Arkansas has been wearing its belt tight, after all, since it just barely qualified to be a state in 1836.)

Arkansans still have big dreams and big plans, as Clinton revealed last year in an inaugural address that to many people seemed an inspired American invocation.

"In the recent past, we have learned again the hard lesson that there are limits to what people can do," Clinton said. "Let us not learn too much of this lesson, however, lest caught in the thrall of what we cannot do, we forget what we can and should do. We are people of pride and hope, of vision and skill, of vast capacities for work.

"We have the prospect, for which we have waited so long, of economic growth which does not require us to ravage our land and so to reject our heritage. We have the immeasurable benefit of living in a state in which the population is sufficiently small and widely dispersed for people of all kinds still to know and trust each other, still to believe in and work together for the elusive common good. We have an opportunity together to forge a future that is more remarkable, more rich, more fulfilling to all Arkansans than our proud past, and we must not squander it."

—

Altheimer (207 alt., 494 pop.) was founded as the headquarters of the Altheimer brothers' plantation in 1883. A typical
cotton town, it contains gin, commissaries, stores, and
homes strung along the parallel highway and railroad track.
—WPA Writers' Program,
Arkansas: A Guide to the State (1941).

Deep in the Arkansas Delta, the roads south straighten out into
ruled section lines, and heavy, cottony clouds join the lint and the
sweet burnt-graham-cracker smell of cottonseed mash in the roiled
air. Here there is cotton, genteel diction as traditionally southern as
anything in Georgia, and old whitewashed homes that once aspired
to be the magnoliaed mansions Arkansas planters were never rich
enough to build.

There are only a quarter as many farms in Arkansas now as there
were immediately after World War II. New high-technology
agribusiness operations have catapulted Arkansas into the position
of the nation's leading producer of rice, its fifth-largest producer of
cotton and seventh-largest of soybeans. Enough chickens are raised
on Arkansas farms to feed the entire United States, yet the state still
ranks fourth in the percentage of people living in poverty.

In Altheimer, there's plenty of poverty. The town sits in the fields
of the eastern part of Jefferson County, at the western edge of the
Delta. It is off the highway now, or at least it's off the one most people use. Its distance from the main road is said to be the problem or
the excuse for its problems, depending on whom you ask. Skinny
dogs sit in the middle of the road that runs through Altheimer and
seldom bother to look over their shoulders for traffic. The place re-
veals that mean, rusty glint, that hiding-rodent skittishness that
derelict railroad towns take on after a while. Old black men—most
of Altheimer's residents, who currently number 1,034, are black—
sit on splintered benches under Main Street's corrugated iron

awning. Some of the old men tip their caps and nod as if they know you, and a few of them move toward the edge of the raised, old-fashioned sidewalk, as if they were going to step off for the white man just like they used to.

Altheimer is hardly the empire my ancestor Louis Altheimer had in mind when he declared, toward the end of his life as a pioneer, that Arkansas had been kind. And Arkansas was certainly less than kind to his son Maurice Altheimer, my great-grandfather, a sober, scholarly man who was called back from his law firm in St. Louis by his father to run the plantation.

When my grandfather's sister brought her "up East" fiancé down to Arkansas to meet her future in-laws, the young man stepped off the train in Little Rock as a truck sped by dragging a dead black man by a rope strung around his neck. White people stood on the platform talking about a white girl and a church belfry. (It later turned out they'd lynched the wrong man.) Maurice immediately took the young man down to Altheimer to show him the plantation. In his office, Maurice told his future son-in-law that due to floods, drought, boll weevils, market prices, and his periodic loans to the black sharecroppers, the plantation in Altheimer lost some $10,000 a year.

"Why don't you give this shit back to the Indians," young Bernie said. Uncle Bernie had gone to Princeton. Maurice was crushed.

Altheimer, Arkansas, today is just as it has always been over the 43 years since Maurice's death—a recalcitrant, revanchist little cotton town. One thing that kept Altheimer so perfectly preserved in Arkansas's murky amber was its longtime sheriff Pink Booher. ("Oh, what a pretty pink baby!" is the inspired comment said to have produced Booher's Christian name.)

Pink's law-enforcement methodology included letting it be known in Altheimer that he was after someone and suggesting a time and place where he expected to meet the individual. Pink had notches on his gun.

"You know, this wasn't always such a quiet little town," said George Martin, the black principal of Altheimer High School. "You lay down and slept at night only because Pink Booher was around." Before I left, Martin rather formally announced that there was "something I ought to know" and proceeded to tell me that there were black Altheimers living in Arkansas. I knew that, of course. My family never tried to hide my great-great-grandfather's penchant for loving all the women of Arkansas.

According to everyone I talked to in Altheimer, Pink Booher's praetorian stance was struck at the behest of the Elms Planting Company, which had once been owned by my great-grandfather Maurice. Today, the frog in the puddle of Altheimer, Arkansas, is one Dick Barnett, former overseer for a distant Altheimer cousin and current president of Elms. I asked Barnett, a man who over-enunciates "bull-ack pee-poe" and slips into "niggah" on the back half of his sentences, what he planned for the future of Altheimer.

"Oh, Altheimer?" he said. "Altheimer's just a dirty ole cotton town that's about to dry up an' die."

Pink Booher died a few weeks before I arrived in Altheimer, after more than 40 years of keeping Altheimer as mean and ugly as possible. A black woman in Altheimer smiled when I asked her about Pink's demise. "The good Lawd finally helped us out on Pink," she said.

I had already spent a good deal of time studying the new face of Arkansas, so Altheimer was more of a personal jolt than a threat to the model of hope for an inhabitable future that most places in Arkansas appeared to embody. The juxtaposition of permanence and change consistently shed illuminating sparks at every bend in the road, and Altheimer would remain, long after my Arkansas travelings, a symbolic counterpoint to the general direction of the state. Old things just seem to stick around down there, and Altheimer serves as a dusty monument to Louis Altheimer's time. Whatever latent force maintained Arkansans' fierce independence and the sheer exuberance of their public life also preserved a bit of the old violence, the Justice Jims and Pink Boohers. The skeletons still protrude at times, like the old Civil War bones after a rain.

—

Even monuments weather, however. A child named R. Walker grew up on a plantation outside of Altheimer and went to town every Saturday to buy candy on Altheimer's Main Street. When his stepfather died, R. moved across the Arkansas River to Pine Bluff, a railroad town filled with ex-sharecroppers in an age that has left railroads and sharecropping behind. Then R. left Arkansas—because he was a black man who wanted to get on in life. But after college and ten years in the Marines, R. heard that things were changing back home and decided to return. The upshot is that the current Pine Bluff city council is referred to by more than a few residents of varying color as seven idiots and R. Walker.

R. Walker—just R. ("Nobody's goin' nowhere in politics with a name like Roosevelt")—ran for his city council seat against a loud, gray-haired white man named Fred Condrey, who tended to pronounce "Negro" as "nigra" and who had been on the council for 16 years. In the words of one Pine Bluff political observer, "R. just waxed Fred Condrey's white ass."

R. ushered me into a small office in the grocery store he runs and took off his red baseball cap. There was a Styrofoam "R. Walker" hat on the wall alongside a picture of John F. Kennedy and another of Martin Luther King, Jr. "There are still a lot of dark ages behind us here," R. explained. "There are still bad racial attitudes in some areas of the city, but basically people understand now that the socioeconomic problems here transcend racial barriers."

In early February, R. strode into a standing-room-only meeting at the city hall and announced to a stomping and clapping interracial mixture of powerful business and community leaders that if he has his way, Arkansas's leadership revolution will soon extend to the old planters' bastion of Jefferson County—because, R. told them, he plans to be their first black mayor. "I'm what you call a maverick, I suppose," R. explained before his announcement, in his deep, dignified voice. "They like mavericks around here these days, 'cause a maverick is one who don't sing in the choir."

R. smiled wide when he said that. People like R. Walker and Bill Clinton, the young immigrants and the generation of young natives that has decided to stay home, all smile at the prospect of being so close to the creative restructuring of a society strengthening itself. As for me, I felt some of the immigrant excitement of Louis Altheimer: there was an almost tangible absence in Arkansas of the cynicism that pervades the more advanced sectors of the society I'd come from.

Exploring Arkansas, with its hillbillies, lizards, and hippies in the hills and its Clintons, R. Walkers, and even Altheimers on the flats, is like exploring an American cultural ark. I found the most ambitious and least ambitious people I'd met in a long time within a few miles of one another in Arkansas, all of them reflecting in their own way the near euphoric thrill of feeling themselves a part of something new.

Above all, there is the continual sound of a scraping and scratching down through the sedimentation of a painful and tragic history toward something that is still magnificent about America, toward some yawning, pristine American purpose. The abiding respect for old-fashioned gumption, the tolerance for human eccentricity that allows Granny Friars and back-to-the-landers with Ph.D.'s to live happily in the same hollow, are not so far from the qualities that sent dreamers and pioneers to Arkansas in the first place. The simple popular belief that things are going to get better and the presence of politicians who still think that the role of government is to promote the general welfare are wonderful anachronisms in these times of Jerry Brown diminutions. There is "hope," as Bill Clinton would have it, that has overcome that legendary power of Arkansas's fears.

So I came back north, where health and freedom are promised by a more expensive pair of polyurethane wheels on one's roller skates. I'd arrived in Arkansas with tales of forgotten hills—which I found. I had also brought with me tales of hate—of which I found only the hollowest of echoes. I left with some new tales for the folks back in Illinois about the state that always stumped you on the geography test, about how an immense, unbridled promise still lives down in Arkansas like a miniature national dream.

GEO, June 1980

THE "MISDEMEANOR MURDER" OF
JOE CAMPOS TORRES

Last May, six members of the Houston Police Department turned a noisy drunk named Joe Campos Torres into an unlikely martyr. As he entered the Club 27 bar on Houston's rough east side the night of May 5, Joe Torres was simply a man who was about to camp on the wrong site.

At Club 27 they'd seen how Joe got when he was drunk. Once, he'd taken off his shoes and announced that his hands and feet were weapons. He was one of those quiet people who got tough and confident when he was drunk. When the cops arrived, he reportedly rose to his full five and a half feet and offered to displace an officer's Adam's apple with his toe. They say that the karate ("Tae Kwan Do," he always corrected) and drinking were to compensate for the fact that Joe Torres was a small man, shy around women and painfully aware of the limitations of an eighth grade education. He'd been in lots of fights, but nobody had ever seen him win one.

When he was in the Army he'd once tried to assault a truck and broke his hand. Once the MPs found him in a forest, high on glue with a garbage can over his head, and another time, he went into town and took on four Fayetteville, North Carolina, policemen. He told his father that the military police had often beaten him with nightsticks. Eventually, the Army and Joe Campos Torres decided that America could defend itself without Joe's help.

After his discharge, Joe came back to Houston. He was living with his grandmother and waiting to get a high school equivalency certificate so he could apply for a job with the phone company. People close to him knew that his real ambition was to open a karate school.

It's not clear how much Joe already had under his belt when he came into the Club 27 last May, but the owner seems to have decided that Joe had had enough to pin him to the pool table and call the cops.

It may have been because of something he said or, as they later claimed, because he was "kicking at the windows" of the police car, but the two policemen who came to get Torres decided that his attitude toward them warranted stopping off on the way to jail to "talk some sense into him." So they arranged to meet the four other cops who'd arrived at Club 27 at a parking lot to conduct the conversation.

Everyone in the Chicano community knows that Houston cops regularly take people to dark alleyways or deserted warehouses to "teach them respect," "calm them down," or "educate them." Mouthing off to a member of the Houston police force goes beyond macho. It's loco.

When they got to the parking lot they dragged Joe out of the car and threw him onto the gravel. Then five of the six stood around him in a circle.

Torres' father had been born in Houston and neither he nor his son had ever been to Mexico. But the policemen still called Torres "Mexican"—"stupid Mexican." "Hey Meskin," they said, "you gonna whip our asses now?" Then they proceeded to beat him, kick him, hit him with a pistol-steel cased flashlight, and throw him around by his handcuffs.

When they finally got him to the jail, the duty sergeant took one look at Joe and told the cops to take him to the hospital.

Instead, they drove Torres back to the scene of his beating. One of the cops dragged his prisoner out of the car and over to a ledge high above the Buffalo Bayou. The "bah-oh" was a beautiful stream before the good citizens of Houston realized that the other major cities in the world are ports. They proceeded to turn part of it into the Houston Ship Channel, a malodorous trench, hidden by highway overpasses, that everyone fears may someday catch fire.

"Let's see if the wetback can swim," other cops had heard Terry Denson say on their first trip to the bayou. Then, according to fellow officers, Denson, a 27-year-old Marine veteran, a former football letterman, a member of a national high school honor society—a big man who was many things that the 23-year-old Torres could never be—did something that would make himself and the bellicose drunk in his custody famous. He threw Torres into the bayou.

Several days later the cops would contend that they'd asked Joe if he could swim and that he'd said he could before he went in. Some of the cops say they saw Joe doing the backstroke in the dark water, but others say they saw him sink. None of this mattered to Margaret Torres, because last Mother's Day she got a phone call and was told that her son's bloated body had been found floating in the Buffalo Bayou.

The five policemen decided to say that they had taken Torres to the hospital and forgot about the whole thing, but the one who had stood away from the beating, Carless Elliott, couldn't stand it. Elliott was 20 years old and had been a cop for only a few weeks. He proceeded to do the undoable. He filed a report and subsequently testified against members of the Houston Police Department, breaking a code of silence that has allowed the force to operate without interdiction or restraint for many years.

When two of the six cops were indicted for murder, many Houstonians expressed shock at the arrogance with which their police consistently abuse their power. The cops had been beating and often killing people in the name of justice and the Houston Chamber of

Commerce for a long time, but there had always been more pressing, profitable things to worry about. There was something in the nature of Joe Campos Torres' rotten luck that had finally hit a nerve.

—

Some people had been outraged back in 1971 when a reputed drug addict named Bobby Joe Connor was stomped to death. They were reminded of the Connor case last year when two members of the department spotted a 27-year-old black man named Milton Glover walking down the street looking "wild-eyed." Glover had sustained head injuries in Vietnam, so neighborhood people tended to ignore his incessant sidewalk preaching. When the cops told him to stop, Milton made his last mistake. In the words of one police officer, he "went for" his Bible and drew it from his pocket. They shot him eight times.

Then, early this year, there was the 17-year-old longhair who was supposed to have threatened police with a gun when he emerged from a stolen van. An eyewitness said on television afterward and contends to this day that the kid was unarmed. The witness says officers threw him on the ground, leaned over him, and shot him in the back of the head.

Right after that the Houston way of justice extended to a right-side-of-the-tracks white man named Sanford Radinsky who made the mistake of being wealthy, young, a reported user of popular drugs, and in bed with two women at the same time. On the pretext that he was making pornographic films, 16 Houston policemen in flakjackets stormed his hotel room one night and killed him. The police said Sanford went for a gun, but the women in the room said that he didn't.

People talked about the wino the cops found in a tire store a few days after Radinsky's death. One cop shot him 13 times after he reportedly attacked with a small pair of scissors. The cop said that he shot so many times—even stopping to reload—because it was dark. "Hell, chief," the joke making the rounds in Houston law-enforcement circles went, "two more bullets and I could have written my name."

None of the policemen involved in these incidents was charged or disciplined. Within the past four years, nearly 30 cases of Houston policemen shooting civilians in similar situations have been heard before local grand juries, after which the policemen involved have been "no-billed"—let off entirely.

This isn't supposed to be happening in Houston, Texas. Houston was in the middle of its process of "coming of age." It's "energy city," "space city," "the golden buckle of the sun belt," the modern boomtown that boosters continually point out has the healthiest urban economy in the world. Because of a hilltop east of town called Spindletop that suddenly started gushing black stuff back in 1901, and with a lot of help from multinational corporations, the National Aeronautics and Space Administration, Arab money, Lyndon Baines Johnson, and the subjugation of its minorities, Houston was on its way to becoming the great American city. But its frontier, cow-town legacy remained too close to the surface for a city that was entering the international executive suite. In 1971, the activities of the Ku Klux Klan still made the front page (some Klan members, at the time, turned out to be Houston policemen). So the town fathers all agreed that it was time for an image change if Houston was truly to reach gleaming perfection in the seventies.

In the wake of the killing of Joe Torres, however, Fred Hofheinz, the 39-year-old mayor elected in 1973 as a symbol of the new, reformed, more civilized Houston, a Rhodes scholar and lawyer who holds a Ph.D. in economics, began spouting some of the most fearless badmouthing that had been heard in the homelands since General Sheridan declared to his troops at Fort Clarke, Texas, in 1855 that if he owned hell and Texas, he'd rent out Texas and live in hell.

Hofheinz announced publicly that he believed there to be "something loose in this city." He spoke of an "illness," "an attitude that supports the police no matter how mistaken they are," and a system that makes "every cop a king." Hofheinz knew from the start that any change in Houston would run up against the blue-clad custodians of the prevailing social structures and racial attitudes, neither of which has changed much since the ancestors of Houston's present aristocracy tamed the frontier during the last century. Yet he persisted in talking about a "frontier mentality . . . where police are given pistols and firearms and given complete backing by the white leadership of the community." He said this phenomenon had "its roots in racism" and was based on a belief that "you need the police to keep things the way they are."

Hofheinz began to tell friends that he was fed up. He told them that he wanted to move to Europe.

—

"So you the Yankee writer come down here to see how we teach our Meskins to swim," one of them observed with a smile. Then the other people at the table laughed.

One of Houston's largest outdoor beer gardens seemed an unlikely place to talk about what had happened to Joe Torres.

Hundreds of healthy, clear-faced couples, many of them in cowboy boots and hats, stomped around the dance floor doing the "cotton-eyed Joe," while others lined up to take a wallop at an old-fashioned strength tester. Every once in a while someone would emit a stentorian *"eeeee-yaaaaaa-whoooo"* as if he meant it.

I took another sip of beer and stared up at a young man called Catfish. Catfish had warned me that his attitude was bound to be conspicuously pro-police since he was a five-year veteran of the Houston Police Department who had only recently left the force for a better-paying job.

Catfish said that the whole Torres thing was "nothing more than a case of minority causin' trouble." He told me in all sincerity that the policemen who'd beaten Joe Torres had made only one major mistake and that was involving six policemen instead of two. "You never do that," he said. "There were too many mouths around and one of them talked."

"You don't even hear about the daily stuff," Catfish said, "but people get pushed around all the time. You don't hear about it simply because people know when they've done wrong. You find that people usually accept their punishment on the street. You just got to discipline them sometimes."

Catfish had never thought about whether or not it was a Houston policeman's role to punish people. An attempt to ask him what the cops thought of things like courts and Constitutions only served to heat up the dialogue.

"Did Joe Torres accept his punishment?" I asked.

"Hey, you know what Torres did?" he snapped. "He was cursin' them boys out and callin' them pigs. I hear he spit in those officers' faces. Would you let a Mexican spit in your face?"

I asked him if he'd read any of the comments that police officials in other cities had been making about how the Houston cops are trigger-happy. Catfish kept staring at me with a rather sardonic look which implied that our conversation was becoming superfluous because of my inability to understand how things are.

"Look," he sighed. "Look," he said, "if you pull up in front of a store and you see two niggers running out of it with a shotgun—now you know they probably just killed somebody inside. What are you gonna do? I ask you. You gonna yell, 'Stop, niggers, or I'll shoot'? Hell no, you waste 'em."

Catfish spoke nostalgically of onetime Houston Police Chief Herman Short, the man who is credited with retaining the old virtues and making the HPD what it is today. Short was once mentioned by George Wallace as the man who would possibly be his FBI chief after Wallace became president. "To tell you the truth," Catfish said above the whooping and staccato clomping of heavy-heeled boots, "I think Herman Short is the best thing since God's bread. If the Torres thing had happened during Chief Short's era you can bet that it would never have seen the light of day."

Herman Short did, in fact, bring a lot of new methodology and philosophy to the Houston Police Department. It was discovered, for instance, that the criminal intelligence division had been keeping some 1,000 personal files on people like Congresswoman Barbara Jordan, the current mayor, and most of the "liberal" community leaders in town. One of the files was marked "Miscellaneous Niggers." Short's department wiretapped at will. According to sources in the Texas legislature, the police kept records, referred to as the "Fag Files," which contained photographs of local gays in various sexual positions. The sources contend that the Houston police did, and still do, take gays they've arrested to a certain warehouse and force them to pose. The police have been known to receive cooperation from major film processing outlets in Houston. If anyone brings a roll of film to be developed with any nudity in the photographs, copies are sent to the Houston police. At a recent meeting of the Texas State legislature committee formed to investigate child pornography, a Houston police official showed up with photos of families sunbathing in the nude in their backyards and submitted them as examples of rampant moral decay.

When people ask about trigger-happy, untrained, pistol-whipping cops, Houston's boosters recommend that those people check out the Houston Police Academy.

I arrived on the day that the man from the gun company was trying to sell the new cadets their first pistols. The new class had been welcomed to the academy the day before I arrived by the chief of police. ("There are no blacks, there are no browns, there are no whites in this class," he told them. "Everyone here is blue.") Now, after 24 hours, they were being told which guns to buy. The Houston cops are among the last in the country who still buy their own guns. It was quite recently that some minor restrictions on what types of guns they can carry were finally imposed. Some of the old guard were apparently partial to high-powered hunting rifles.

Before becoming prospective policemen, the cadets have to prove beyond a shadow of doubt (with the help of a lie detector) that they have never committed adultery, lived illicitly with a member of the opposite sex, or smoked marijuana.

Lieutenant I. L. Stewart, who runs the Police Academy, told me that he was sick of the "stupid Torres thing," but that "nobody supports what was done—even though Torres was a creep, a real creep."

Stewart says that recruits are being trained to be ethical: "We're tryin' to teach them to be unbiased, to set aside the fact that their neck may be red or it may be black or it may be yellow or it may be brown."

He said police work is different from other professions because it involves "discretion." "If I felt endangered by a black person I'd shoot at a black person. If I felt endangered by a white person I'd defend myself and shoot at that white person—same thing with a Mexican person."

Many citizens of Houston appear relatively unimpressed with their police department's egalitarian attitudes pertaining to whom they shoot. The fact remains that they tend to shoot a fairly large number of people. Some 14 civilians have been killed by the police this year during incidents that have been or will be subjects of grand jury inquiry. There are also an inordinate number of "assault against police officer" charges on the record in Houston because this appears to be the charge often handed out to someone who's just been administered "street justice" in the form of a beating. There were thousands of "assault against police officer" charges filed in Houston in 1971 alone. Cabdrivers say that when they get a radio call that instructs them to pick someone up at the back of the Houston police station they expect to get someone's blood all over their back seat.

"You grow up in this town thinking that the police have a James Bond license to kill," State Representative Ron Waters explained. "You learn very young that they are the power: that a Houston cop is The Man. I remember the cops coming out to school and having them impart this whole great power mythology. You come to believe that the cop is the law and you're awed by it."

One of the reasons that the police force remains so inviolable is that to become chief, you have to have been a high-ranking police officer in the first place. According to one of Mayor Hofheinz' political advisers, "It's like saying you can pick a police chief but it has to be Mussolini, Hitler, or Idi Amin." According to Hofheinz: "What you have is a perpetuated hierarchy in the Houston Police Department that is almost exclusively white. There's not a single black above the level of sergeant, not a single one in a city that's 28 percent black. . . . Your decisions are being made over there by one socioeconomic group up and down the ladder who reinforce each other and are protected by the Civil Service Law and there's not a friggin' thing that the mayor can do."

The tradition of the tough lawman is all but indistinguishable from the venerable history of the state of Texas. When a child learns what it means to be a Texan ("We chose this land; we took it; we made it bear fruit"), he finds that the Texan view of the world is constructed upon the deeds of men who assumed and used great power at the jagged edges of the frontier. As he grows up, he may come to notice that the mentality of the frontier has never left that segment of the society protected by Houston's warrior class.

———

My encounter with the opinionated ex-officer Catfish was arranged by one Scotty McClosky. Scotty is a big, blond former Texas A&M football player. He has big, wide Texas features, holds the door for old folks, and flirts with middle-aged "ugly ole bitches" in bars "to make them feel good." He used to date a former Miss Texas. Scotty is a chunk of old Texas, Lone Star, utterly un-self-conscious and secure as hell in his role as a walking hyperbole. To my carpetbag Yankee journalist sensibility, he was perfection. As he cruised around Houston in his big new car, Scotty explained how you can suss out the sociological status of a Texas lady by assessing her "accent and attitude." He honked at most women we passed on the street. "Oh," he said, "they love it."

Scotty's great-granddaddy was at the Alamo. The McClosky family went on to become landowners who had the good fortune of finding oil on their property. This is considered the most acceptable manner in which to have accumulated wealth among Houston bluebloods. At 29, Scotty works occasionally as a freelance undersea engineer for oil drilling rigs and spends a great deal of time trying to avoid being sucked into "daddy's oh-all company."

Because he had lived abroad for a while Scotty seemed able to intuit what it was I was looking for in Houston and seemed to believe that I could find it simply by spending a few days in his presence.

Scotty felt sorry for Joe Torres and agreed that the police force contains "some sneaky mothers" and "some mean bastards" but still sees the force as made up of a lot of kids like himself, me—and Catfish.

Houston is an immense, zaftig city; it's eerily clean and as new and well kept as a stitch-pocket sport coat. New buildings are being "skinned up" everywhere and unfinished bridges and overpasses jut out unexpectedly at every turn. Houston is more than ever a boomtown, the fastest-growing city economically and demographically in the country. The population has multiplied 28 times since the turn of the century and grew by a third between 1960 and 1970. People speak nostalgically about the way Houston looked five years ago and more than one resident has left for six months and not recognized the city upon his return.

Houston simply reeks of new wealth. Some 200 corporations have moved their offices there since 1970. There are restaurants and discotheques that reserve the 30 more conspicuous parking places for Corvette Sting-Rays, all of which must have their wheels turned in the same direction. Scotty and I visited stores doing heavy business in $350 mink cowboy hats and $400 lizard-, ostrich-, or elephant-skin boots. We saw shops filled with ivory tusks, Frederic Remingtons, Russels, and framed collages depicting the illustrious history of barbed wire. With little prodding most white people in Houston will tell you that if you can't make money in that city—you just can't make money.

There is no mass transit. Everyone has cars, mostly the big ones. The traffic is horrendous and the air smells like it does in Gary, Indiana.

"You know what the best time to be in traffic is in Houston?" Scotty said as we sat in one of Houston's inevitable traffic jams. "Well, it's Sunday morning: the Catholics are in church; the Jews are in Miami; the niggers are in jail, and the Mexicans can't get their cars started."

We passed the famous Astrodome, a monument to the limitlessness of imperial supposition such as hasn't been seen since the English Victorians built the Crystal Palace in order to house together everything new and good in the world in the name of Progress. They said that nobody would go out into the tropical summer heat to watch a baseball game in Houston, so Roy Hofheinz, the present mayor's father, went out and built the first stadium replete with a roof, fake grass, and air conditioning.

A Houston criminal lawyer named Phil Green later told me: "Any time this city wants something or realizes that it's missing something it just goes out and gets it. There's none of that 'small is beautiful' shit down here. As soon as you get a mentality that involves limitations—you're finished, this whole country's finished. It's part of everything that's good here, including 'We shall overcome'—do you think that was 'small is beautiful'? Do you think that Martin Luther King would have accepted 'small is beautiful'?"

Green has defended lots of Houston policemen and lots of Houston criminals. He believes that the police department is well suited to the pathological drive toward prosperity that makes Houston great:

"The cops in this city are exactly what we want them to be. They reflect all of the things that cops should reflect in a city like Houston. This is a democracy—believe me. This here is a town of players."

Democracy doesn't seem to be quite the word for the Houston power structure. Houston is one of the last large cities that is still ostensibly a city of town fathers. The governmental relationship of officials to the people is strongly patterned after that of a corporation to its stockholders. It's no accident that many of the city's leading political characters have been real-estate developers or promoters of one kind or another. The city's business elite used to meet in a suite at the Lamar Hotel to figure out how to run the place. The mayor who held office for the ten years preceding Fred Hofheinz is presently the head of the chamber of commerce. His police chief was Herman Short and he just let Herman run his end in his own way. When I asked Fred Hofheinz which segment of the community reinforced the "illness" that allowed the police to run wild, he said, "I think most of the community knows some of the players. It's not one or two, it's an epidemic." Houston is run for profit. A police force full of people who make it known that they are potential killers has rarely been harmful to the workings of laissez-faire commerce—in some countries it has obviously helped.

—

Two months after Joe Torres' death, State District Court Judge Allen Stilley decided that the policemen involved couldn't get a fair trial in Houston and ordered a change of venue to Huntsville, a small town about an hour and a half south.

When Joe Luna Torres, Joe Campos Torres' father, heard that they'd moved the trial to Huntsville, he decided that he wouldn't bother to attend. "I knew what was going to happen. There's nothin' but rednecks out there. When I used to go to work near there the damned kids would all come out and throw rocks at the truck."

There had been considerable pressure before the trial in favor of having federal authorities try the policemen for violating Torres' civil rights instead of trying to make state murder charges stick, but at the last minute, the local DA got the go-ahead from Washington.

The two most notable things about Huntsville are that it houses the Sam Houston State College School of Criminal Justice, where many of the college-educated Houston cops went to school; and that it is the site of the Texas State Penitentiary. The major source of entertainment in Huntsville is the Huntsville Rodeo, in which prisoners at the pen are offered various privileges in return for attempting to survive the experience of being instant cowboys for the entertainment of visitors.

By coincidence, the judge who ordered the trial moved to that particular location had only been a judge for a few weeks. Before attaining his judgeship, Allen Stilley had been Houston's assistant district attorney in charge of presenting the police brutality cases that had for years been thrown out by grand juries who heard them.

During the trial, a former policeman admitted that it was not unusual for policemen to brutalize a prisoner. They spoke of the "code of silence" between officers and about their belief that a good policeman needed a "reputation as a tough guy."

Former officer Glenn Brinkmeyer had been an usher at Terry Denson's wedding, but this didn't stop him from testifying that Denson had deliberately pushed Joe Torres into the bayou. He said that he realized that Torres was sinking in the muck.

After Terry Denson's Baptist minister, his brother-in-law, and his Cub Scout leader had testified to his veracity, Denson announced to the court: "I never pushed him." The spectators in the courtroom booed.

The defense attorneys for the policemen did the only thing they could. They attempted to turn the trial into an indictment of Joe Torres. When the Huntsville district attorney later read the court record, he was overheard to say: "This is a hell of a good case, with all of those police officers testifying we ought to be able to convict that damned wetback."

The all-white jury returned a guilty verdict, convicting the officers of negligent homicide—a misdemeanor. Of the conviction charges offered the jury, they chose the one closest to acquittal. The jury accepted that the cops hadn't meant to kill Torres and never doubted that they had asked him if he could swim before he hit the water. Before they retired to consider the sentence, prosecutor Ted Poe warned them that "by your sentence you will set a price on killing people."

Later that day, it went out on the wires that the jury in Huntsville had decided to fine the two convicted policemen one dollar each for killing Joe Campos Torres. The cops actually received probation for one year and a probated fine.

A prosecutor who had been involved in another case—six years earlier—of Houston policemen killing a suspect, took the fact that the cops were convicted at all as an indication that "perhaps we're becoming more civilized." Prosecutor Bert Graham, who had helped argue the case, was also philosophical: "At least they did convict them. It's the first conviction of a Houston police officer of brutality since Reconstruction—at least they convicted them of something—it's more than we've been able to do in the last hundred years."

———

"Look at them mothers," Scotty said as we drove past the floodlit buildings of the Houston skyline. "Ain't no energy crisis down here, no sir." Scotty had insisted that we hit yet another Houston gathering to get some more opinions from insiders on the Torres case, so we set off one evening for a party at the home of a former deputy sheriff named Doug.

At Doug's house, I witnessed some of the most serious drinking I'd seen outside of certain South London pubs. I also saw something amazing. On one of the walls of Doug's living room hung a formidable semiautomatic weapon. As it turned out, Doug was personally acquainted with the late Joe Campos Torres.

"He was a real asshole," Doug said from behind his belly. "I knew him. I even arrested him once. A real asshole. I'll tell you another thing, I think he jumped in."

"Why would he jump in the bayou?" I asked.

"Outta spite to the police. He was just that mean."

"You mean you think he killed himself to get these cops in trouble?"

"Sure do."

At this point I noticed Scotty peering at me from behind Doug's shoulder. He was winking and grimacing and making all manner of "what-did-I-tell-ya" faces.

We then began to discuss the fine points of the Torres case. "Now there were four witnesses and three of them say that Torres jumped in," Doug resumed. "One witness, that Brinkmeyer, he says different. Now that's three against one. Who you gonna believe?"

"Well," I said, "after reading the record, I tend to believe Brinkmeyer."

At that point Scotty hooked one of my belt loops and dragged me over toward the hors d'oeuvres table. "Hell, man," he whispered, "don't you come up against a Texan in his own house like that. Just agree with a Texan like that, don't go mouthin' off."

I strode back toward Doug and resolved to try another subject. I began to look around the room. "Hey Doug, is that a semiautomatic up there on your wall?"

"Yep," he said.

"Wow, does it work?"

Doug's face began to flow around his cheekbones. His jowls tightened and pulled back, and with a seemingly mechanical movement hoisted his lower lip up toward his nose. "I wouldn't have it in here if it didn't work," he hissed.

Scotty had moved several feet away from Doug and was holding his head with both palms. "Whoa shit," he said, "you're gonna go down right here. Oh hell, let's get out of here."

As we got in the car I kept asking Scotty what year it was and he kept talking about "stickin' his neck out for nothin'."

"You know, Don," he said as we drove back toward my hotel, "I like you 'cause there's a unique thing about you, you got a unique thing that no other Yankee who comes down to Houston has."

"What's that?"

"A plane ticket home."

—

After the Huntsville sentencing, there were rumors of planned violence and scheduled illegal marches by Chicano groups. People put up signs that said RACIST COPS and KILLER COPS. Others appeared in public wearing dollar bills on their lapels—a reference to the jury's assessment of the worth of Torres' life. Striking workers on the picket lines at the Hughes Tool Company screamed "Murderers" at the cops. The Torres case has provoked Houston's relatively docile minority community into a flurry of organized activity. Before the trial, various groups had been forming committees and occasionally marching to protest police activities. But after the sentence was reported, the Chicano community got hot.

Mexican-Americans in Texas had been strenuously mobilizing

against police brutality for some time; especially since the trial of a Castroville, Texas, sheriff who had blown a young Chicano's head off with a shotgun in 1975. The jury in that trial sentenced the sheriff to two to five years. Pressure from Texas Chicano leaders subsequently motivated U.S. Attorney General Griffin Bell to issue what is now known as the "Bell Memorandum" earlier this year. The memo instructs local U.S. attorneys as to the conditions under which federal prosecution should follow state prosecution concerning the same incident. The federal government retired the Castroville sheriff and found him guilty of depriving the dead Chicano of his civil rights. He was sentenced to life imprisonment.

A contingent of Houston Chicano leaders went to Washington after the Torres verdict to try to get Bell to indict the six Houston cops. While they waited for an answer, there was more talk of people arming themselves. The police force went on emergency control.

State Representative Ben Reyes was one of the community leaders called in to meet with the recently appointed police chief, Harry Caldwell, about the tense situation:

"The whole experience was somethin' else—the climate of that meeting—he told us that he didn't want this thing to get out of hand. We said, 'Shit, neither do we. We understand what's out there.'

"Then he says, 'I want you to know that we got the fire power and when it comes time to get down to the streets, I'm gonna use that fire power.' Then he says—and this scared the shit out of me—'If there's a confrontation, I expect to lose two men.' My immediate reaction was, 'Hell, if he's losing two, I'm gonna lose 20.' "

Reyes shuttled between Houston and Washington where he attempted to pressure the Justice Department into quickly indicting the policemen on civil rights violations.

Ben Reyes came back to Houston after a year and a half with the Marines in Vietnam having lost one lung in combat. He found that "everything was still the same. My folks still lived in the same four-room house and my brothers and sisters were dropping out of school." Reyes eventually decided to run for the state legislature from the predominately Chicano Magnolia District. Joe Torres made campaign signs for him.

I asked Reyes if he thought that Terry Denson had asked Joe Torres if he could swim.

"Hell, no," he said.

While middle-class Houston was beginning to feel an uneasiness, twinges of fear, and a great deal of embarrassment over the uncontrollable nature of their public servants, individuals involved in the minority communities were becoming increasingly radical.

Jack McGinnis, a Catholic priest from Beaumont, Texas, had received a frenzied phone call from one of his parishioners last March. "They got Demas in the front yard," he was told. McGinnis went out and witnessed the logical conclusion of the occasional phenomenon of a young black man trying to outrun the Houston police. Demas Benoit had led 20 police cars on a chase that ended in front of his home. The police proceeded to handcuff him and, in front of Benoit's parents, slam his face against some concrete, kick him, and perform knee-drops on his back. As Father McGinnis approached the scene in horror, a young policeman came up to him and said, "I want to tell you that I tried to stop them. I want you to know that we're not all like that."

The police inquiry ended up ignoring Father McGinnis' testimony ("They lied about the whole thing," he says. "When the report came out it said that I hadn't seen a thing") and completely discredited the young policeman who had filed his own account of the beating. In fact, the police inquiry committee recommended that the young cop be fired for leaving his post. The report said that the police had to beat Benoit's head against the concrete because he was biting one of the officer's fingers. A well-documented article by Tom Curtis that recounted some of the activities of the police force in *Texas Monthly* magazine later reported that the policeman's finger had in fact been bitten by a mental patient in a hospital several days earlier.

"I'd known about it for a long time," Father McGinnis says. "I'd get three calls a week from people who'd been beaten up by the police. Finally, after 14 years, I saw the tail end of something. I sat back for the whole weekend afterward thinking, 'I'm not going to sit here. If I have to burn myself on the police station steps, I'm not going to do it.' "

McGinnis proceeded to do something that people in Houston had never seen before. He went on a 31-day hunger strike and thus succeeded in keeping the beating of Demas Benoit in the newspaper every day.

"It's more than a frontier mentality down here," McGinnis says. "It's racism out and out—just flat-out racism."

"Do you think they asked Torres if he could swim?"

"I don't think so," he said.

Texans have a history that is conspicuously devoid of problems with minority groups. The Plains Indians couldn't seem to toe the line when the frontiersmen first arrived, so they were exterminated. The Mexicans were conquered with a bit of help and have only been allowed back to fill certain labor gaps, and the black population was imported to become slaves and lived together on the outskirts of various Texas towns. They pride themselves in Houston on never having experienced major racial violence.

In 1967, the police actually seized the local black college, Texas Southern University, an act that eventually led to a shoot-out. The leader of the TSU chapter of SNCC was then arrested for passing a joint to an undercover cop and sentenced to 30 years in prison. The man, Lee Otis Johnson, is presently in jail on a different charge and under consideration by Amnesty International for listing as a political prisoner.

Then in July of 1971, the Houston police force blitzed an entire black neighborhood in what, even in the light of police action in other cities in the last ten years, is remembered as an unprecedented show of force. Hundreds of blacks were beaten and arrested as police stormed the Third Ward of Houston, with helicopter support. There was no apparent provocation. Somehow in the darkness, Carl Hampton, the leader of a nascent organization that was later to become the local branch of the Black Panther party, was shot in the head and killed. "It was a horrendous display of police brutality," said State Representative Mickey Leland, who was beaten and arrested at the time. "It was as if all the police brutality that had been exercised undercover for so many years had finally been put in one place for a night."

"They came out with so much fire power in such force," one observer says, "that the black leaders just said, 'The hell with this.' "

"The cops are the frontiersmen who're shooting away to wipe out all the Indians," Leland believes, "and it works. It's not necessarily to annihilate them, but to corral them, to keep them on the reservation, to control them.

"You know, when Fred Hofheinz became mayor he put the squeeze on them in the beginning. Hofheinz was a progressive man; he did a lot for the black and brown community, but he never really addressed the police problem because he couldn't."

———

When Fred Hofheinz came into office he immediately set out to repay the debt he felt he owed the black community who had helped elect him (he received 95 percent of the black vote). Hofheinz tried to bring in a new police chief named Carol Lynn to clean the department up. Lynn managed to expose some of the department's illegal wiretapping operations before the machinery within the department geared up to subvert him. His top aides began to ignore his orders. Cops would get off the elevator whenever Lynn would get on—he was rocking the boat. He was eventually replaced by a man appropriately named Byron "Pappy" Bond.

"They've been out to get Fred Hofheinz ever since he started to go into politics," said State Representative Ron Waters. "I remember the first time he ran for mayor, the time he lost. The police showed up at his election headquarters after the results came in and towed away all the cars."

After his attempt to curtail the police department's power, political observers in Houston naturally assumed that there would be open season on Fred Hofheinz. Meanwhile, his attempts to budge the conservative monolith made up of the city fathers became increasingly frustrating personally to the mayor. "I'm gonna stand up in the council and just throw up one day," Hofheinz told National Democratic Committeewoman Billie Carr, a well-known Houston-based political strategist. "I've got to get out or I'm gonna blow my cool and they're all gonna burn me." Last June 9 Hofheinz announced that he would not run in the November mayoral election.

"They" finally burned Hofheinz when it was mysteriously leaked a few days after his decision not to run again that a "high city official was being investigated by a grand jury over something having to do with his morals. The rumors hit the streets and spread through Houston like an oil fire. The city's small town roots are never more evident than when there's gossip to be disseminated. Hofheinz, people whispered to one another, had either been found with another woman, found with another man, arrested in a coke raid, arrested in a gay bar, or arrested in an after-hours club. The most lavishly embroidered version of the story was, of course, Scotty's.

"Ya see, they raided this gay bar and found this beautiful chick in the back givin' a blow job to a guy who runs one of the big clothing stores around here. They were snorting coke and all. So they take this chick down to the police station and fingerprint her. Then a little later the sergeant comes running out and says, 'That's no girl, that's Mayor Hofheinz.' "

A grand jury, convened to investigate the allegations, found them to be totally without substance.

"You have to understand that they did the same sort of thing to his father," Billie Carr explained. "They even tried to impeach his father and what happened to him was hovering over the whole thing. Fred's attitude now is, 'Fuck it, if that's what the city wants, then, fuck it.' "

—

A few days after hearing that the two policemen charged in their son's death were given suspended sentences, Joe Luna and Margaret Torres were sitting at Zippies, a pinball hall near their home. Mr.

Torres looked out into the parking lot and saw a policeman holding a gun to the head of a young Chicano. The irony hit Torres immediately. He ran into the parking lot with a pool cue in his hand.

"Hey man," Torres said to the cop, "what you got that gun up side his head for? That ain't right."

The policeman told him to go back inside before he got in trouble.

"Look," Torres said, "my kid got killed a few weeks ago and if somebody had said something when they dragged him out he'd be alive right now."

Then Torres told the boy in the policeman's custody to report the cop's license plate number to the local FBI office. It was at that point, according to the Torres family lawyer, Percy Foreman, that the cops "lit into Mr. Torres" with their flashlights, threw Mr. and Mrs. Torres and their two young children into the car, and arrested and jailed them for resisting arrest.

Joe Luna Torres grew up in Houston at a time when Mexican-Americans received an average of a third grade education and rarely rose past a service job with the city. He's a big man. In the Magnolia District they used to call him "Apache." "I've been picked up 17 or 18 times by the police and have been beaten every time. My head's all full of stitches," he says. "A lot of my friends have been killed by the cops."

Percy Foreman is one of the most famous trial lawyers in the world. Foreman once defended 13 women accused of murdering their husbands in one year and got them all off. He was also the defense attorney in the trial of James Earl Ray. Cynics say that he has become a rich man because the wealthy folks of Houston are forever killing each other.

Foreman's grandfather and father were county sheriffs. One brother was the head of the Texas State Highway Patrol and another was a DA. He has a son who's a Galveston policeman. Foreman has defended many policemen as well as entire departments. But lately Percy Foreman has taken to calling the town he's lived in for 50 years a "police state" and has compared the civil conditions to those of "some totalitarian states."

Foreman believes that the consistent whitewashing of brutality charges by Houston's DA office is to blame for the Houston cops' disproportionate accumulation of power. "If there's no control over them, if they're given blanket power, they'll react just like the KGB or the Brown Shirts or any other totalitarian constabulary."

—

Finally, on October 20, Attorney General Griffin Bell announced that indictments had been returned in Houston against four of the five cops involved in the Torres case. The fifth was named as an unindicted coconspirator. The charges included various violations of Torres' civil rights. The maximum sentence involved is life.

The announcement tended to mitigate some of the tension in the minority communities; other people resented the federal intervention. The police chief welcomed the news. One of the more amazing aspects of the Torres case is that the department believes the aftermath of the killing to be their finest hour. Cops look at you with the righteous eyes of a spanking parent and say, "We cleaned our own house."

Congressman Donald Edwards, chairman of the House subcommittee on civil and constitutional rights, an ex–FBI agent and the first member of Congress to begin to monitor the Torres case, says that he will consider calling hearings concerning the Houston Police Department if the same kind of information that came out in the state trial emerges in the federal proceedings. "These are federally protected rights," Edwards says, "and we're not about to let any community go outlaw."

People speak of the irony of the federal intervention. Someone in Washington had finally implied to some people in Houston that they must respect the civil rights of a lost and frustrated Chicano who six months earlier had died without a touch of dignity.

Streetwise Joe Torres never would have thought that his death would move things around on the other side of the tracks. The federal trial of his killers will commence after the first of the year and Percy Foreman will undoubtedly make the upcoming trial of Torres' family on charges stemming from the incident at Zippies worthy of considerable public notice, but many people have found out the hard way how things really work in Houston since they found Joe in the Buffalo Bayou. Among them there's the black high school student who had been taken hostage and killed when police approached the car he and his abductor were in, filling it full of bullets; and the 16-year-old boy who was hiding in a small bathroom of a liquor store he had broken into and was killed when a cop swung open the door of the room and shot into the darkness, hitting the unarmed boy in the chest. One of his accomplices, a 13-year-old girl, was found behind the store with getaway bicycles.

Fred Hofheinz says the police in Houston are now "an institutional monster with police power." His remedy is to put the mayor in a position of power sufficient to control the personnel on the force. Many Houstonians believe that a state civil rights statute would help. There is talk of a civilian review board to monitor the police or the appointment of a special prosecutor (some people want to retrieve native son Leon Jaworski), but the pressure toward these ends is minimal.

Despite the brief outcry after the death of Joe Torres, the nature of the police force is rapidly devolving as a palpable issue in Houston. Mainstream Houston will remain at peace with their primordial lawmen as they will with their rampant pollution, paralyzing traffic, bad water, and some of the smelliest sewers in the hemisphere. "We don't have so much time for our friends and neighbors, for each other, for our families," Percy Foreman figures. "There's so much opportunity here that the work ethic being what it is—we are just, all of us, more concerned with our individual fortunes than we are with the community."

Texas lawmen have been shocking non-Texas observers for a long time. At the turn of this century people wondered about Texans when the mostly Texan Rough Riders celebrated their victories in Cuba by roping black men on the streets of Washington, D.C. The disproportionate status, power, visibility, and old-fashioned barbarity of Houston's contemporary warrior class will probably recede only when the battered, nearly comatose sons of members of the chamber of commerce, or the friends of people like Scotty McClosky instead of the friends of somebody like Joe Torres are thrown in the Buffalo Bayou to see if they can swim. Many people fear that the whole "Torres thing" will become a signal for a new crackdown, because every once in a while they do choke on their prosperity down in Houston—but usually they manage to clear their throats.

"This is a city of niggers and nice folks, cops and robbers, assholes and elbows," lawyer Phil Green had explained. "People get crude here. If you stayed here long enough, you'd be a crude writer." Green kicked his heels up onto a big desk and turned away as I stared into the leather and glass hinterlands of his lavish office. He stared into the lustrous southern sunlight for a moment, then swiveled his smile in my direction. "Look," he said, "that's just the way it is."

Rolling Stone, December 29, 1977

INSIDE L.A.'S NEWEST POWER CLUB

O ne recent evening 40 Los Angeles residents in the throes of young success were invited to an elegant cocktail party at the Regency Club. Though many older members of the city's corporate establishment had been relegated to a waiting list, officials of the elite six-year-old club had carefully culled an assortment of rising functionaries of the city's professional firms and invited them to the antique-lined clubhouse 18 stories above the corner of Wilshire and Westwood.

"You ever been here before?" a young employee of the investment bank Goldman, Sachs inquired of a young Salomon Brothers banker.

"Only once," he responded. "For one incredible closing dinner."

"Me, too," said the Goldman, Sachs man. "Best end-of-the-deal meal in town."

The candidates for membership wandered down the parqueted central hallway and peeked into one of the club's smaller rooms, where Drexel Burnham Lambert heavyweight Michael Milken had a few days earlier chosen to lunch away from the public eye. In another, a few days before, the notably aggressive banker Joseph Pinola had been introduced to the notably aggressive airline executive Frank Lorenzo. "You are to be congratulated," the leader of First Interstate Bancorp was overheard to say to the leader of Texas Air. "You are one of the most interesting people around." It was in one of the smaller chambers back in 1984 that the creator and owner of the Regency Club—David H. Murdock—looked up after a big lunch and declared to Dr. Armand Hammer, chairman of Occidental Petroleum, that Hammer was too old to run Oxy and that he—Murdock—wanted his job.

Twenty-six leaders of Los Angeles' 50 largest industrial companies are members of the Regency Club. Thomas V. Jones, chairman and chief executive officer of Northrop Corporation, does most of his business entertaining at the club. Lew Wasserman, chairman and chief executive officer of MCA, and Sanford Sigoloff, chairman and C.E.O. of Wickes, are seen there often with associates. Many of the 956 members say they belong to the club, which has no golf course, tennis court, or swimming pool, just to have access to its cuisine. Some cite the convenience of being able to show up at a good restaurant without a reservation, while others admit to relishing the sound of their own names when they exit from an elevator. But many members made their applications, risked rejection or relegation to a waiting list, and ponied up the $5,000 entrance fee in response to precisely the same natural tropism that has drawn the powerful and wealthy together into the contrived enclosures called clubs for centuries.

The truly great private clubs of history were spawned during periods of social transformation and economic activity. The leaders of colonial empires created private clubs that often evoked an idealized sense of the mother culture the colonialists had left in order to gain the very status they were now underscoring by forming clubs. Early in this century, the burgeoning economies of U.S. cities caused people to form clubs, as each wave of new achievers sought to distinguish their level of attainment. Over time, those kept out of the older clubs on the basis of sex, ethnic origin, religious preference, method of financial attainment, or the relative length of time one's money had been in the bank seemed more important to the invented tradition than those allowed in.

The Los Angeles of 1981—the year the Regency Club was opened—still contained two examples of these turn-of-the-century preserves. The downtown California and Jonathan clubs, with their hushed plutocratic decor and Maalox-smooth cuisines, retained images of being haunts of gentlemen possessed of significant municipal bond portfolios and modestly Anglo-Saxon surnames. The downtown "power palaces" still seemed to define the old downtown/Westside dichotomy—the divide between old money and new, Christians and Jews, and gray-haired white men and everyone else.

The vogue in starting private clubs had ostensibly died out toward the middle of the century, as most of the movers and shakers of the post–World War II surge seemed content to integrate themselves into the downtown clubs or the Westside country clubs instead of starting their own. A few newer country clubs were built, but somehow the pervasive big-power aura of the urban eating clubs is diffused by talk of golf handicaps. There really hadn't been a new power palace in Los Angeles for many decades by the early eighties, so leading members of the community were surprised to get calls from friends about a new club start-up. They heard that the Regency Club would be different from the clubs to which they belonged, if for no other reason than that its conception and execution sprang directly from the powerful mind of David Howard Murdock.

Then 58, Murdock—real estate developer, corporate takeover artist, Republican Party power broker, horse breeder, arts patron, orchid-grower, and all-around man of considerable wealth and taste—was said to have told his friends that the day he dropped out of the tenth grade back in Ohio, he already knew he possessed an uncanny knack for making money. Murdock dug ditches and flipped burgers at a little joint he bought outside of Detroit before he headed toward Phoenix to build some small houses, then some big ones, and then some office buildings that still dominate the skyline. He lost most of this money during the early sixties real estate slump, made some of it back, then came to California in the mid-seventies to enhance his assets by developing more real estate and acquiring companies. Recently, he has expanded his fortune by using the tactic of *almost* taking over companies whose leaders decide to pay him "greenmail" so as not to be acquired. Such was the case with Murdock's move on Occidental Petroleum: Hammer and Oxy had to pay Murdock $60 million (others say it was $100 million) for Murdock's stock and his agreement to abort his takeover attempt.

By the time he decided to found the Regency Club, Murdock had acquired a huge ranch in Ventura that was home to his collection of several hundred Arabian horses, and he'd purchased one of the finest homes in Los Angeles—a 64-room mansion in Bel-Air built by Conrad Hilton. There, he and his late wife, Gabriele, gave lavish parties attended by Californians whose great-grandparents settled the region. Though ubiquitous at society functions, Murdock remained something of a mystery to the general public as well as to those who did business with him or attended his parties. He was quoted once in *Fortune* magazine as saying that it was "useless to give money to the poor because they only lose it." Because he said he was quoted out of context, and in the end could gain little from further press exposure, Murdock has been wary of interviews ever since. But in a sophisticated yet inexorable way, Murdock had managed to insinuate himself profoundly into the economic, political, and social life of the city at a pace only Los Angeles would tolerate. By 1981, he decided the city needed a new sort of club.

He'd been a student of private clubs for some time when he decided to build one atop Murdock Plaza, his new red-brick and dark-glass office building in Westwood. He'd already put private dining clubs on top of his buildings in Lincoln and Omaha, Nebraska, and he'd built the exclusive Cloud Club on top of one of his high-rises in Phoenix. But Los Angeles—as open as it might have been to the newly wealthy—was still a long way from Omaha. The downtown elite already had their hidebound clubs, and Westside residents had their beach and golf clubs.

But Murdock would not be dissuaded. "The Regency Club will

have a single prevailing doctrine," he declared. "To be, quite simply, the finest club in the city."

"I just closed my eyes," he remembers now, "and I thought, 'What kind of club would I like to have, would my friends like to have, and would their friends like to have?' "

One night Murdock invited a disparate group of powerful Los Angeles residents to a meeting at his home. Present were such noted Democrats as then–party chairman Charles T. Manatt and attorney Paul Ziffren. Entrepreneur John E. Anderson was there, as were Tom Jones, Roy L. Ash, Joe Pinola, and Peter V. Ueberroth. Also attending—in their own right, and not as stand-ins for their husbands—were Mrs. Armand S. Deutsch, Mrs. Harry Wetzel, Mrs. James L. Stewart, and Carole Scotti, sister of Lieutenant Governor Mike Curb. "This club will be open," Murdock told his guests, "and women will be eligible for full membership."

As long as you could pay your bills and knew five members willing to attest to your good character, Murdock seemed to imply, then you too could join an elite urban eating club. The exclusivity of the club would be predicated on wealth and reputation instead of criteria related to birth or creed. The idea struck Murdock's guests as novel in the extreme. It was contended in the press before the club opened that Gabriele Murdock was behind the open membership policies, but, in fact, the urban, all-male bastions were already under siege.

The Jonathan Club's failure to extend an honorary membership to Mayor Bradley—a tradition apparently denied the mayor because of his race—had never ceased to be an issue, and the court cases pursuant to Rotary International's decision to expel its Duarte chapter when it admitted women went back to 1978. When William French Smith was nominated to be attorney general at the end of 1980, he was widely criticized for his association with an institution as clearly discriminatory in its policies as the California Club. Murdock was too good a businessman not to see what was coming. "I saw that there was a new, aspiring America out there," he says now, "and I believed the days of closed doors were past—they never should have existed."

Murdock's admissions policies attracted attention. Prominent downtown attorney Kendall R. Bishop of O'Melveny & Myers had previously declared to his partners and friends that he wouldn't attend a firm-related function at the California or Jonathan club. Bishop was vociferously "anti-club" in general, but he joined the Regency. Ueberroth realized that he could hold organizing functions leading to the 1984 Olympics at the Regency without having to worry about the sex or race of his guests.

Another unusual aspect of the Regency Club, Murdock announced, would be that it would be run as a business. Unlike most clubs, which are owned cooperatively by their members, Murdock would own and operate the club and underwrite its start-up costs (about $5 million) himself.

———

From the beginning, Murdock made it clear that he envisaged a club of active, vital members, not an institution dedicated to the care and feeding of dinosaurs. This, he said, called for good food, a subject about which Murdock was known to have strong and rather idiosyncratic ideas. Murdock ate five meals a day, each of them rich in protein. Employees who didn't eat a proper breakfast while traveling with him were given stern lectures about the importance of protein to the functioning of the mind. He believed that, with the exception of the meals at the Hillcrest Country Club, the food served in elite clubs was by and large pedestrian, and he didn't much care for any of the restaurants in Westwood. The Regency, he vowed, would serve gourmet food of a quality rarely seen in Los Angeles' best restaurants.

Murdock hired chef Louis Outhier, owner of the three-star L'Oasis on the French Riviera. He then went to the Carlyle Hotel in New York in search of a club manager and lured away veteran professional Giorgio Masini. He hired a publicist, one-time New York gossip columnist Wally Cedar, and he told Cedar to promote the Regency Club as he'd promoted the Four Seasons restaurant in New York for many years. Most of the early planning and staffing was handled by none other than H. R. (Bob) Haldeman, who had come to work for the Murdock organization shortly after serving a prison sentence that grew from a previous and less successful management experience. Upstairs at the new club—one floor above the Murdock organization's executive offices—Haldeman was known as the "chief of staff."

While Murdock delegated numerous duties to his team, he insisted on approving every detail—particularly any detail that involved color or form or taste. Since he had recently purchased the venerable London and New York antique dealers Stair & Co., a ready source for period antiques was available to fill the 15,000 square feet of the club. The only individual to whom Murdock yielded on matters of decor was his beautiful, German-born wife, Gabriele, whom he considered to have an instinct for design detail not unlike his prodigious instinct for combining assets. Gabriele Murdock said they wanted to create a club that could be like "an extension of their private homes" to members, a place they could go to "feel secure."

For their part, the Murdocks chose to live in a formal manner that most members of the upper classes had cast off 50 years earlier. Their home was extremely formal, and David Murdock's personal style was formal to the point of parody. Murdock believed in dressing for dinner—in dressing for breakfast or lunch, for that matter—so anyone who wanted to be a member of his club, he declared to would-be members, was going to have to wear a coat and tie when they came around to eat.

———

Today, some members still complain about the strict dress code at the Regency Club. Board members bring it up at meetings, and Murdock hammers it back down. But at lunch one recent Friday, everyone in the opulent dining room was dressed in accordance with management's standards. Julian Zelman, the developer and County Art Museum fellow; Emil P. Martini Jr., chairman and C.E.O. of the Bergen Brunswig medical-supply corporation; the consul general of

Saudi Arabia; and Stephen D. Moses of the Democratic Party, who had recently brought John F. Kennedy Jr. to lunch, were all well-dressed, and they all made entrances with a formality and grace of which Murdock might have approved. Murdock wasn't yet sure whether he would take the corner table where he likes to sit and "see everything that goes on," so he remained at work in his office on the floor below.

At one of the prized window tables, Joseph Baird, the former Smith Barney investment banker and one of the many short-lived presidents of Occidental Petroleum, was having lunch with Joseph F. Alibrandi, chairman and C.E.O. at the Whittaker Corporation and a member of the club's board of governors. "I just never went for the old English men's club atmosphere," Alibrandi said. "This place has a cross section of people with different points of view. There's no Great Divide between old and young here, but then I'm not a club guy. I think of the staid, more exclusive clubs as places where people who are exactly the same get together. My wife calls the old clubs elephants' graveyards."

"Oh, I don't know," Baird said to his lunch partner. "I like other clubs, too. It's not a crime. I belong to the L.A. Country Club, the Bel-Air Country Club, and the California Club."

Alibrandi looked shocked. "Well, it's certainly not my thing," he said.

The politics surrounding private clubs have heated up considerably in the years since the Regency Club was founded. As Murdock foresaw, restricted country clubs and men's clubs have been forced to alter their policies profoundly within the last few years, but not before publicity and public hearings sponsored by the Los Angeles City Council managed to mark the old downtown clubs in particular as embattled refuges for an endangered species.

As the call for litigation and further reforms at the other private clubs has increased, the Regency Club has appeared ahead of its time. There are about 100 women in the club now, though most appear to use it for social rather than business purposes. A few, such as Joanna Carson, ended up with membership by virtue of divorce settlements. There are only a few Hollywood celebrities—among them Arnold Schwarzenegger (who is said to have written a fan letter to Murdock before he was admitted), Kenny Rogers (the spokesperson for Dole Pineapple, a subsidiary of one of Murdock's companies), and actress Barbara Carrera (who is married to the son of a Greek shipping magnate, the Drexel Burnham Lambert banker Nicholas Mavroleon). There are three blacks: O. J. Simpson, U.S. District Judge David W. Williams, and James N. Harding, owner of the Jim's Barbecue chain.

Far from a melting pot, the Regency Club is a delicate simmering of the closely similar. "It's certainly not a case of open admissions," says J. Clayburn La Force, dean of the Anderson Graduate School of Management at UCLA and chairman of the club's membership committee. "We are looking for honest, hard-working, respectable people. We discriminate, I guess, against the slobs."

After a recent Friday lunch, Stanley A. Wainer, chairman of El Segundo–based Wyle Laboratories, approached Bonnie Kyle, the club's managing director, to tell her that he was going away for several weeks. Wainer is an active member who recently held his daughter's wedding at the club. But on this day he seemed slightly perturbed over not having a window. He told Kyle he was going out of town and said something about saving his table.

Kyle smiled and wished him bon voyage. "Nobody can have their name on a table here," she said after Wainer left. "But making all of that kind of stuff work out is part of my job. These are people who are used to getting their way, but people at the top are still the best to deal with. They aren't paving their ways up to the top anymore, so it's easy for them to be nice."

Kyle, a 35-year-old Texan who held other jobs under four different Regency Club members before coming to the club, has been the managing director since 1985, when Giorgio Masini went to work at the newly opened Manhattan Beach Country Club. Before that, she was the assistant managing director. The chef overseeing the kitchen this lunchtime also began his career, in 1981, as an assistant at the club, but since then, Joachim B. Splichal has become one of the city's culinary stars and is now a consulting chef at the Regency. (Splichal left the Regency Club in 1983 to open the Seventh Street Bistro, and then moved on to the well-reviewed but poorly situated Max au Triangle as chef and owner. After Max closed, Splichal served as a consultant to QV, the old Quo Vadis in New York, but had come "back home" to the Regency for a short stint at the helm.)

Splichal, a dapper 31-year-old German who trained in Europe under the legendary Jacques Maximin, says that cooking at the club requires certain adjustments. Rather than employ his genius for creative cuisines, for one cholesterol-conscious member Splichal had to make omelets with only the whites of the egg. Another wants warm toast with Parmesan cheese on top, slightly burned. Sandy Sigoloff likes his potatoes crisp. Armand Hammer (not that he comes in so often since the day Murdock told the good doctor he was over the hill) likes a certain fresh tomato sauce on his pasta. For his part, Murdock is a fan of pork and lobster in champagne sauce. David Buell, chairman of Metrobank, comes in for lunch every day to a salad of string beans, chicken, and mushrooms with a bit of vinegar on top. The mere thought of the "Buell salad" makes Splichal's lips curl. But in the end, the food at the club has been a salient factor in its rapid success. Murdock brought world-class chefs into the city during the early days of a culinary renaissance that has catapulted Wolfgang Puck, Michael McCarty (a member), and Los Angeles cuisine in general to international acclaim. The club is considered to have been the training ground for some of the city's best chefs, and it remains the source of some of the city's finest food. The recently hired executive chef, Franck Champely— late of Maxim's and Taillevent in Paris and the Pierre in New York— is expected to continue the tradition.

Food is the centerpiece of several of the special events staged for club members under Bonnie Kyle's direction. But Kyle has also tried to enhance the social side of the club. It has sponsored several events in a near-Victorian spirit of self-improvement, including etiquette courses for young children under the direction of protocol expert and erstwhile White House advance person Alyse Best. One of the most popular special programs was called "A Return to Salon Days," in which an English professor came to the club for four evenings of poetry reading and group exegesis of Coleridge, Shakespeare, and Yeats.

—

Though Kyle manages the special programs, the general theme of highly mannered, carefully choreographed connoisseurship that pervades them derives from Murdock. Murdock is a reader, writer, and recorder of poetry, for instance, and some of the members still talk of the time he showed up at one of the salon evenings and read his favorite poems in a fine, clear voice.

When Murdock enters the club for lunch, he tends to go straight to his corner table without saying hello to members. "I eat there a great deal so I can make certain that everything is done properly," Murdock says in the clipped, careful way he speaks. "I talk about the menus, the wine, and so forth. I insist that all our silver be spotlessly polished all the time. If you pay attention to every detail and have great people—Bonnie Kyle is a wonderful manager, for instance—then the club will work."

Even when Murdock is not physically at the club, his presence is apparent. Kyle will often send memos down to his office at his Pacific Holding Company headquarters on the 17th floor that inform him of particularly important guests who are due for lunch; occasionally she even suggests that it would be nice if he came up and said hello. Kyle also appears to spend some of her time covering for Murdock's habit of walking by people, lost in a fog of thought. But most members seem to accept that Murdock is one unusual fellow and that, for all practical purposes, they have been invited to *his* dining room. The club is not theirs; it's his, and if he seems a bit abstract at times, that's not the end of the world. "In most cases you'd resent the situation," says Stan Wainer, "but in this case, he deserves to call it his. He decorated it. He created it. He owns it. It's his club."

A private elevator descends from Murdock's club to a hallway leading to his office, a shrine to one man's adoration of elegance and "lovely things." The towering walls of the huge office are covered in glowing wood exhumed from the inner floor joists of English buildings constructed when George IV served as regent and king. A museum's worth of antiques divides the office into many different seating and working areas. H. R. Haldeman, who has seen many of the great offices of the world, says Murdock's office is better than the late shah's working quarters in Iran and just as good as the two best offices he's ever seen—the one occupied by J. Edgar Hoover toward the end of his reign and the perfectly maintained czarist quarters that are the main offices in the Kremlin.

"I love old Chippendale," Murdock proclaims. "I love old wood.

"I found tradition to be in the way of progress my whole life, and the best thing one can do if you don't like it is to change it. But I'm a very traditional individual as far as aesthetics are concerned. I like old art."

The office is intimidating. It's a sensation that continues as Murdock rises ceremoniously from his desk at the far side of the room. He tends to hold eye contact a bit longer than most people. "He's looking inside you then," Giorgio Masini says. "It's as if he's searching you for the truth." Murdock's heavily starched cuff is embellished by a cuff link bearing a large roaring lion's head as greenish and aged as any weathered public monument. He's wearing one of those heavily tailored double-breasted suits that crosses rather high upon the chest, and because it is 4 in the afternoon and the garment remains unmarred by the slightest hint of a wrinkle, it appears as if Murdock hasn't taken a seat all day.

Since inviting the elite of Los Angeles to join his club, Murdock has been busy conducting the most profitable business ventures of his career—a series of financial assaults that have marked him as one of the most aggressive of the corporate raiders. He has so actively taken to combining assets, developing those assets, taking over companies, and occasionally selling companies that his personal stake in the various entities he controls is valued at more than $700 million. Murdock carries a business card, etched in an antique script not unlike his Declaration of Independence–style signature, that reports his control of several substantial American corporations.

Shortly after opening the Regency Club, he acquired most of the textile manufacturer Cannon Mills and recently sold much of it at a huge profit. A 20 percent stake in Iowa Beef Processors Inc. (now IBP) was parlayed soon afterward into $135 million worth of Occidental Petroleum shares when Oxy absorbed Iowa Beef. Murdock eventually accumulated $250 million in Oxy stock, which allowed him to join Armand Hammer on the board. His attempt to oust Hammer two years later produced a considerable profit. When the management of FlexiVan Corporation, a New York transportation-equipment leasing company, tried to oust Murdock from its board in 1983, he wrested control of the company and eventually used his assets to edge out fellow raider Irwin L. Jacobs for control of the venerable Hawaiian-based pineapple and real estate company, Castle & Cooke.

As raiders and greenmailers go, Murdock resides among the gunslingers of big capital as a sort of Bat Masterson, a carefully manicured, even friendly usurper, who is still capable of turning into a "business barracuda," according to Hammer, when the situation warrants. Yet Murdock has also done much to improve the image of raiders and real estate developers, in part by allowing free rein to his abiding passion for "lovely things." The Joffrey Ballet now calls Los Angeles home for part of the year only because David Murdock sank so much money into the effort. Maggie Wetzel and Gabriele Murdock hosted a gala at the Regency Club for both the East and West coast boards of the Joffrey when the deal to move the Joffrey was struck, and Gabriele Murdock was involved in many other cultural and social events that associated her husband's name with Los Angeles' recent drive toward a haute culture.

But in early 1985 Gabriele Murdock died of cancer at the age of 43, and that same year, one of Murdock's sons was drowned in an accident. Friends and associates say that they sense a deep sadness and a greater reserve in David Murdock now. But his determination to brand the ornate "M" worn by service employees at Murdock

Plaza on buildings and institutions all over the country has continued apace.

As he settles back into an antique sofa, Murdock chooses to
speak not of the companies he's taken, but of things he's built, of
things he's made. He's proud of the remodeling of the Hay Adams
Hotel in Washington, the last project that Gabriele helped to deco-
rate. He's building a huge luxury hotel in Hawaii on some undevel-
oped Castle & Cooke property, and he offers photographs of a hotel
he's built on Baltimore's refurbished waterfront. When the subject
of Cannon Mills comes up, Murdock wants to talk about the fact
that he decided to literally tear down the ugly company town of
Kannapolis, North Carolina, five years ago. He rebuilt 1,400 more
aesthetically palatable homes for the workers and paved their sidewalks with red brick. "You'd be thrilled to see the town. It's completely redone with lots of new stores. There's a boulevard down the
center just like Park Avenue in New York. All kinds of trees and
flowers bloom all over, and there are little pushcarts. The town is
just the kind you'd dream about. I just kind of dreamed what I
wanted to see there."

Murdock is not alone in his possession of a fine eye and a highly
developed sense of taste and order, but he is distinguished by his incessant efforts to foist his sense of taste and order upon others in the
form of new economic arrangements, new hotels, new buildings,
new towns, and new places to be, like the Regency Club, where sim-
ilarly powerful people can come together as long as they are willing
to sit in rooms, eat food, drink wine, and even dress according to de-
signs wrought by a fellow who works 30 feet below the carpeting.
Just as achievers in the past constructed great clubs to embroider
physical definition upon their status and privilege, Murdock never
stops reifying the fact of his possessions and power with the constant alteration of the physical shape of things. He is less like Horatio Alger than like the characters in the Ayn Rand novels he's read.

In part because he chose to do it in Southern California, Murdock
was able to build a building, build a club, people it with members,
and have it take on the patina of social prominence in just six years.

Murdock is probably the only living founder of an urban club whose membership represents great wealth and power. The founders whose names appear on the aging brass plaques in the Jonathan and California clubs, in the great clubs in New York, and in the clubs along Pall Mall in London have been dead as long as have the people whose names are on the street signs outside.

At the Regency Club, tradition has been invented and even taught via special classes. Murdock suggests that the success of his club—which he contends is "quite profitable"—is marked not by waiting lists or membership lists or mentions in the society columns, but by the creation there of a common view of the world. "People get together [in clubs] so that they can have an intermingling of thoughts, experiences, and ideas. The people here—when we started it—were a group that didn't know each other. But as time's gone by with all the different parties and all the other things that we've had, it has become such that you have a group of people that have the same ideas in life."

Before he reaches below an antique end table and pushes a button that causes the massive wooden door to swing open automatically, he mentions that he owns 1,800 prime acres near Lake Sherwood. "I'm going to do a whole country club out there," he says. "Creating things—that's my specialty. I love to create things, to start things. I've been doing it for years."

David Murdock was once asked if he would ever run for office. "Why would I?" he said. "I have my own world, don't I?"

———

As the cocktail party drew to a close, the young Regency Club members of the future began to make their way to the elevators as the club's dinner guests began to arrive. The mysterious and powerful Murdock had failed to make the journey in his elevator to shake their hands, but still, most of the aspirants felt that they'd had valuable chats with members of the admissions committee. Within a few weeks, more than a dozen of them would submit their applications.

In choosing the Regency Club as the name for their new club,

David Murdock and his wife recalled a period of English history during which an appreciation of fine dress, beautiful furniture, and the higher arts was rekindled after a long hiatus. London was completely rebuilt by John Nash—"re-done," as Murdock says of Kannapolis—and Regency dinner tables were the scenes of nine- and ten-course meals of a quality that hadn't been witnessed anywhere since the time of the Roman Empire.

But only in America, during the last quarter of a singularly active century, could a fellow who once slung hash at a greasy spoon near Detroit pursue his Promethean aspirations with such brilliance and energy that he one day could tell some of the most powerful people in the world that they have to wear a tie to eat in his elegant dining room—*his* dining room, an expanse commensurate with his own sense of what he's capable of controlling. And only in Los Angeles, California, would these people think for a single second that, all things considered, this was okay with them.

Los Angeles Times Magazine, September 20, 1987

Acknowledgments

Acknowledging the help and support of the many individuals who have touched my life during the time these stories were written is an impossible task. So I will limit this long list to the names of wonderful editors and a few others who offered editorial input.

I once wrote a story for *Outside* about a man who trained hounds to chase raccoons up trees. One thing the man posited was that "you only get one really good dog in a life." There have been times when I would apply this apothegm to editors. In truth, however, I've had many extremely talented editors. I have worked with editors who helped draw from me in conversation what I really meant to convey, editors who knew enough to reel me back from stylistic overreaches, editors who could recast specific lines into a superior balance, and editors who knew when to leave well enough alone; I have even had a few editors who could offer insight into what was missing from a piece of writing instead of homing in on what was already there.

Very much afraid I'll forget someone—and please forgive me if I have—I would still like to thank Jane Amsterdam, Aaron Asher, Mary Bahr, Keith Bellows, Jonathan Black, David Blum, Dominique Browning, Mark Bryant, Betsy Carter, Bob Christopher, Bill Colson, Will Dana, Ken Danforth, Judy Daniels, Christine Doudna, Barbara Downey, Lee Eisenberg, Dan Ferrara, Rob Fleder, David Hirshy, Laura Honhold, Joy Johannessen, Peter Kaplan, Jon Karp, Michael Kinsley, John Koten, Anita Leclerc, Susan Lyne, Clifford

May, Gregg Mitchell, Phil Moffit, Jim Morgan, Adam Moss, Mark Mulvoy, Dan Okrent, Marty Peretz, John Rasmus, Paul Scanlon, Gene Stone, Amanda Vaill, and Jann Wenner.

I have been lucky enough to have two supportive literary agents, Elizabeth McKee and Amanda Urban. I have had a longtime research librarian who helped me—Mark Padnos—and a short list of brilliant early-stage readers of drafts who helped immensely along the way, among them Fred Smoler, Peter Petre, David Blum, Paul Hawken, Jean Kidd, and the toughest reader of them all, Leslie Larson.

Web Resources Directory

Audible, Inc.
[http://www.audible.com]
Esquire
[http://www.esquire.com]
Library of the University of Texas at Austin—map collection
[http://www.lib.utexas.edu/maps/index.html]
Los Angeles Times Magazine
[http://www.latimes.com/print/magazine/]
Outside
[http://www.outsidemag.com]
Ralph Steadman's website
[http://www.ralphsteadman.com]
Rolling Stone
[http://www.rollingstone.com]
Worth
[http://www.worth.com]

About the Author

DONALD KATZ is the author of *Home Fires*, which was nominated for a National Book Critics Circle Award; *The Big Store: Inside the Crisis and Revolution at Sears*, winner of the *Chicago Tribune* Heartland Prize for Non-fiction; and *Just Do It: The Nike Spirit in the Corporate World*. His most recent book, *The King of the Ferret Leggers and Other True Stories*, was published by AtRandom.com. He is a contributing editor for *Rolling Stone* and has been a contributor to *The New Republic, Esquire, Outside, Sports Illustrated,* and *Men's Journal*. His work has won and been nominated for several National Magazine Awards. Katz is the founder of Audible, Inc., the leading Internet provider of spoken-word audio.

About AtRandom.com Books

AtRandom.com books, a new imprint within the Random House Trade Group, is dedicated to publishing original books that harness the power of new technologies. Each title, commissioned expressly for this publishing program, will be offered simultaneously in various digital formats and as a trade paperback.

AtRandom.com books are designed to provide people with choices about their reading experience and the information they can obtain. They are aimed at communities of highly motivated readers who want immediate access to substantive and artful writing on the various subjects that fascinate them.

Our list features expert writing on health, business, technology, culture, entertainment, law, finance, and a variety of other topics. Whether written in a spirit of play, rigorous critique, or practical instruction, these books possess a vitality that new ways of publishing can aptly serve.

For information about AtRandom.com Books and to sign up for our e-newsletters, visit www.atrandom.com.